My Teacher *Is My* Hero

TRIBUTES TO THE PEOPLE WHO GAVE US KNOWLEDGE, MOTIVATION, AND WISDOM

EDITED BY SUSAN REYNOLDS

Aadamsmedia

AVON, MASSACHUSETTS

Published by
Adams Media, an F+W Publications Company
57 Littlefield Street, Avon, MA 02322. U.S.A.
www.adamsmedia.com

ISBN 10: 1-59869-792-7
ISBN 13: 978-1-59869-792-6

Printed in the United States of America.

J I H G F E D C B A

Library of Congress Cataloging-in-Publication Data
is available from the publisher.

This publication is designed to provide accurate and authoritative information
with regard to the subject matter covered. It is sold with the understanding that
the publisher is not engaged in rendering legal, accounting, or other professional
advice. If legal advice or other expert assistance is required, the services of a com-
petent professional person should be sought.
  —From a *Declaration of Principles* jointly adopted by a Committee of the
  American Bar Association and a Committee of Publishers and Associations

Many of the designations used by manufacturers and sellers to distinguish their
product are claimed as trademarks. Where those designations appear in this book
and Adams Media was aware of a trademark claim, the designations have been
printed with initial capital letters.

This book is available at quantity discounts for bulk purchases.
For information, please call 1-800-289-0963.

I lovingly dedicate this anthology to my brother,
Roy Joseph Reynolds,
who spent his life teaching elementary school
students and made the world a better place for it.

Also to my sister,
Rozanne Reynolds,
who taught in a Montessori nursery school for many years.

And, as always, to my beloved children,
Brooke Sandon Aved and Brett Allen Aved,
who will forever be my greatest teachers.

Contents

Acknowledgments

I would like to thank a few truly inspired teachers who made a real difference in my life, including Joseph "Peace Corps" Hnatiow, Mrs. Charlotte Jewart, Alex Peters, Jan Berry Kadrie, Norma Jaichima, Terra Mizwa, and Ron Zak. At Adams Media, I'd like to thank Paula Munier for her impeccable judgment, invaluable editorial direction, endless enthusiasm, and generosity in helping birth projects; project manager Brendan O'Neill; editorial assistant Sara Stock; and everyone else involved at Adams. Also, a special thanks to *Cup of Comfort* editor Colleen Sell for offering her mailing list and many kind words; Brian Thornton for sharing his list; my nephew, Gregory Reynolds, for creating my Web site in a rush; Greg's wife, Shelley Reynolds, for sharing him during those stressful weeks; Emma Gordon and Paula Munier, two of my dearest friends, for coming through at the last minute. And, of course, the fifty contributors who shared their touching stories for all of us to enjoy! Thank you for honoring the teachers who inspired you and now enrich all of our lives.

Introduction

Teachers come in all shapes, sizes, and specialties. A teacher isn't always someone who earned a degree and shows up at school every day urging you to crack your books and work hard to achieve the highest grades. A teacher can be a coach; a music, art, writing, or photography instructor; a mentor; a beloved relative; a close personal friend; an acquaintance; someone you meet on a journey; a shaman; or even a student who turns the tables. But all teachers have one thing in common—they nurture the light they see shining brightly in others and often give selflessly in order to do so.

The best teachers are fabulous characters—full of spitfire and vinegar—who love what they do and convey enthusiasm for learning, respect for responsibility, and a certain *joie de vivre*. Most have unusual conviction and a sense of moral imperative—they believe in your potential and will do whatever it takes to unearth it and set it ablaze. The best teachers teach us indelible lessons about life and how to live it. Unfortunately, even the best teachers may not receive the accolades they deserve, at least at the time services are rendered. Often we don't recognize their real contribution until many years later, when that one small voice continually resurfaces and rescues and guides and inspires us—over and over and over.

This anthology was designed to honor everyday teachers as the true heroes or heroines they most certainly are in our lives. These fifty stories contain tributes to a wide assortment of characters—from a Vietnamese man who scribbles English words on scraps of paper to memorize later; to a crusty Tennessee cowboy who nurtures and guides a young Indian writer 8,000 miles away via the Internet; to a feisty, tough boxing instructor who slips pearls of wisdom in between the punches to comfort a healing woman; to a middle-aged New York City "Jewish mother" who nurtures a struggling Australian actress while they both battle cancer; to an arthritically crippled piano teacher whose love for the instrument and the art inspires another to assume her legacy; to a Chinese tutor who survived the darkest days of Chairman Mao and lived to recount a thrilling history; to a physics teacher who blows up a voltmeter in secret after-school lab sessions to help a struggling math student find his place in the world; to a tough coach who teaches a freshman that loving a grandmother who develops dementia is more important than being a tough guy.

Stories range from the 1940s to the present and cover the gamut from elementary school, to junior high, high school, college, post-graduate school, technical school, and tutoring. Art, piano, music, writing, boxing, and coaching are all included. Stories came in from Canada, India, Australia, Nova Scotia, and virtually every corner of America. Each teacher is a hero or heroine to the student who writes so eloquently about the gifts he or she received at the hand of a master. In homage to the art of teaching, each story uplifts, touches, and inspires. I absolutely fell in love with all of these teachers, these stories, and I hope you will, too.

As you read, I also hope the stories will rekindle fond memories of the teachers who affected your lives and inspire you to write a testament of your own. All teachers deserve respect, recognition, and gratitude. All teachers are heroic in their aspirations, and many are absolutely heroic in their everyday actions. I know I wouldn't be where I am today without some incredibly dedicated, inspired, and memorable teachers. And working on this anthology brought them all back to life, as if they were marching through my living room, dropping by to see how far I've come, and—quite appropriately—bursting with pride for concrete evidence of their good work. Teachers everywhere, cheers to you!

Enjoy!

Pearls, Kings, and Geeks

Lyndell King

The year I turned thirteen, my mother took everything of value from our northern Brisbane house and cleared out. That didn't include me or her alcoholic husband. Needless to say, I was angry, and as any teacher knows, that's trouble in a tatty skirt, looking for somewhere—anywhere—to come unraveled.

Not surprisingly, my thirteenth year included frequent trips to the headmistress's office, albeit interspersed with occasional moments of academic brilliance. Very occasional. And rarely productive. Being the smartest kid in class didn't help one iota because I intentionally used my powers for evil. I majored in mischief and mayhem, practicing them on a daily basis. If authority figures yelled at me, I knew I existed. Mission accomplished.

My teachers seemed torn about how best to deal with me. Some tried to mother me, which I didn't want. Some tried to bully me—for my own good—which I wouldn't allow. Some tried to ignore me—hoping I'd go away. Only I didn't. I had nowhere to go and a truckload of angst weighing me down.

Enter onto the battlefield one unlikely hero in the form of a nerdy ancient history teacher, armed only with life experience and an armada of patience. Fortyish, chubby, and balding, Mr. G. still lived with his mother. He squinted behind Mr. Magoo glasses, brought his tuna-sandwich lunch in a brown paper bag every day, and thought style could be found in a cotton checked shirt, brown tie, and baggy beige trousers. *Of course* I ridiculed him! Unmercifully. Here was another adult I could use to salve my bleeding ego, a ready target for the pain darts I threw at anyone who came near. And geez, he made it all too easy.

Except, upon closer inspection, something was different about this geek. He refused to be rattled by my worst behavior. For one thing, he took all my not-so-clever jibes in stride, mostly with a quiet half smile, giving the faintest hint that he was genuinely amused. He seemed like he knew something I didn't, and he guarded it so that only the very special would be enlightened. Was that on purpose? A tease? A bait? A trap? How much underhanded psychology did this guy know? Fearing I'd underestimated him, I kept a wary eye on this unflappable creature. Everyone had a weakness—that much I knew. I'd keep jabbing until I found his Achilles heel.

I mean, the guy was a totally brilliant teacher, even I couldn't take that away from him. When he recounted graphic stories about the Spartans, they came alive. His eyes glowed with contagious excitement that even I couldn't resist. He'd actually traveled to all the ancient lands they forced us to study, and he brought in his personal slides to bring those cultures back to life. Secretly, I slavered over these fantasy worlds, fascinating people, and the puzzles of political intrigue he shared. I found myself more desperate to hear his stories than to wag class. He gave me something to look forward to each day, something my dull, gray life needed desperately. An escape.

Plus, without making some gross fuss, he gave me kudos for behaving myself. He nicknamed me Athena, Goddess of Wisdom and War. When he brazenly used that handle in class, he smiled that sly, half-smile tease, which was his way to get me to fire up my brain cells and use them in discussions. Sure, I acted affronted, but in truth, I was pleased that he noticed me enough to allot that concrete identity, which even I could see suited me pretty well. In time, I wanted to live up to that name, to be fearless and annihilate all opponents with my verbal arrows rather than sneaky evil acts. I imagined myself as a goddess of an ancient civilization that valued creativity and culture. Wow! I really got into that stuff.

Soon I dreaded the sound of the bell that signaled the end of his class, and I often hung back to argue points with Mr. G, excited when he battled me like an equal. He borrowed books from the university library to share with me, giving me access to things that I'd never known existed. Soon I turned up early for class, keen to see what he'd brought for me, and soon after that I never missed a lesson. By focusing on and evaluating mistakes others made throughout history, he taught me how to use anger as positive energy. Yeah, I wanted to learn that.

And then one day, he gave me my gem-studded crown. It was one of those lunchtime detention classes where we all sat around looking tough and bored, doodling on our hands with pens. He pulled out a competition-sized chessboard, cocked a cheeky eyebrow in challenge and goaded me to play. Then he had the audacity to beat me! Suddenly all my pent-up aggression had a purpose, my devious mind had a positive goal. Mr. G became my Gandalf, empowering me to slay enemies, actually trusting my intelligence and character to ultimately triumph over evil.

He wanted to pit a team from our rundown public school against the immaculately suited private-school kids who'd grown up sniffing gold dust and being chauffeur driven to every kind of after-school club imaginable. When he told the principal he wanted to take his ruffians to the interschool chess tournaments, the guy thought Mr. G was dreaming. So did we. But Mr. G dealt in dreams. He needed a fourth board for his chess team. I was it. My aggression fit the job. So he took the anger I didn't know how to control, and he shaped it into something beneficial—to others and to me. That's the kind of genius that shambling, half-blind ancient history teacher possessed.

Little did those mindless yuppies-in-training know that Mr. G armed his Greek gods and goddesses with piercing armor, ironclad strategy, and a do-or-die creed. Like the Spartans, we trounced them and left them gasping in disbelief. Our school not only entered the interschool chess tournament, we won that year! Who'd have thought it possible? Certainly not me.

During the workup, while I was honing my strategy skills, positioning pawns and castling kings, Mr. G used the chess rules to teach me about the pawns you can afford to sacrifice if it gets you ahead in the game. About the king (secretly a symbol of your heart's desire), which you must guard with everything you have. About the interplay and strength of teammates working together to defeat a common enemy. And how, when you lose a game, you can always rack the pieces up again, take the hard-earned lesson in hand, and fly in the face of life— stronger, smarter, and more determined to win next time.

Yes, I graduated junior high, top of my class—and without a juvenile record. Halleluiah! Everyone was pleased with the final outcome. But it might not have happened that way if Mr. G hadn't hoisted up his baggy trousers and worked his magic. That man sneakily wrote his name across my heart, and imparted wisdom that stayed with me long after the historical facts he'd labored so hard to teach faded. But, lucky for us all, then and now, Athena, Goddess of War and Wisdom, became the powerful woman he let her be. He gifted me with pearls of wisdom, the strength of a king, and the heart of warrior. In doing so, he gave me the world.

Lyndell King is a midwife and naturopath. She sold artwork through the Museum of Natural Art, married an ER consultant, mothered two gifted children (one of whom was Tasmania's under-nineteen composer of the year) and is currently a successful romantic comedy writer, under the pen name of Babe King.

Lucius Publius Wilson

Charles Dickson

It was Mr. Wilson's practice to hear Latin translations while standing at the classroom window, roll-book in hand, looking down the hill at the band practicing.

One bleak winter afternoon, a heavy drizzle of rain began. He recited, "It rains, and the wind is never weary . . ."

Then he said, "You know, boys, it sounds a lot better in German," and he recited the whole poem in German. He made the wind whistle through those harsh enemy vowels of that strange tongue.

After class we pronounced that performance "average," which to us, in 1945, meant simply superb.

He had a Latin joke that he told once or more each semester: A student had a twist of tobacco in his desk. The professor pointed at the desk and asked, "Quid est hoc?"

The student replied, "Hoc est quid."

We stomped and whooped. Mr. Wilson said, "All right boys, it's not that good. You've already heard it from the seniors anyway."

Mr. L. P. Wilson, called "Lucius Publius" by his students, though never to his face, taught Latin and English at Atlanta Boys' High School. He had a great authoritative nose, Roman, and a fine head of gray hair. His glance sparked from behind rimless glasses at any wretched mumbler of an ill-prepared lesson.

When we were scheduled to begin the study of Cicero, Mr. Wilson asked us not to use "horses," an English translation of the Latin. They were called horses because for hundreds of years boys had sat on them and read between their legs for tests or recitations. There were no horses in Mr. Wilson's classroom. There would never be, and he asked us not to use them for study at home. He said we would learn much more by using only a dictionary, working out syntax ourselves.

By 3:30 that afternoon, several members of the class were downtown at Kimsey's old bookstore on Pryor Street. Those who had football practice or ROTC that afternoon had given us money to get Cicero translations. Mr. Kimsey always had plenty of copies because he bought them back at year-end for half price. I found a venerable and serious old horse by Rev. William Judson, copyright 1818. Several other books of translations were by Dr. Yonge, copyright 1851.

One afternoon Hunter was reading, "How long, Oh Cataline must we endure your unbridled license?"

Mr. Wilson stopped the translation. "'License' is too literal for 'licentia' in this case, Hunter. Yonge doesn't always use the best word. Harley, how does Judson have it? I believe you are a student of the good reverend."

"'Audacity,' sir."

"Yes, that's right. You boys are going to have to look at some ice-cold Cicero on the midterm, and I promise you Judson and Yonge will not be here to help you take the exam. It's a shame for your parents to think you are studying while you are sitting there reading those horses. Driscoll, what is this 'virtus?'"

"Ah, 'virtue?'"

"No. 'Courage, valor.' If all you can do is guess a cognate, just say, 'I don't know.'"

One day Harley was reading. Mr. Wilson turned away from the window and shouted "Aiiiieee!" He slid down the wall and sat on the floor. His glasses had come off. He dropped his pen and roll-book. His face was colorless. Several boys rushed to pick him up and sit him in his chair.

He groaned. "It's gallstones, boys. I've had it before. Can someone drive me home?"

He gave Hunter the key to the metal cabinet in the corner. Hunter got Mr. Wilson's overcoat and hat and briefcase.

They carried him by the elbows to the door of the classroom. He shouted in agony. Before he left the room, he pointed at the blackboard and where daily assignments were posted:

Translate: Ullman-Henry, pp. 91 to middle 94.

Grammar: Causal subjunctive. Learn verb "polliceor."

He was back the next day, at the window, roll-book in hand as we filed in for fifth period.

"Okay, Harley. What's the grammar?"

"Casual subjunctive, sir."

"'Causal.' What is its form?"

Harley knew.

"Good."

He never asked any favors from us, but the last week of our junior year he said, "Boys, you are a class of high achievers. You need to keep it that way. I know you are signed up for 'Current Events' for your senior elective. The homework assigned in that class consists of reminders to read the newspaper. I will offer Ovid your senior year. If you take it, you should know there will be no vocabulary to learn, no new grammar. We will just read some of the finest literature ever written. We will critique various English translations. We will critique Judson and Yonge."

That sounded like fun, and it was. More than any college instructor, more than any graduate school professor, Mr. L. P. Wilson conveyed a sense of the meaning—and the joy—of learning. After I completed service during the Korean War, I was undecided whether to accept a fair-to-middling job or to apply for graduate school. I could literally hear Mr. Wilson's voice, "You boys are high achievers. Keep it that way."

I continued my education courtesy of the G.I. Bill and enjoyed a long academic career, thanks to my hero, Mr. Lucius Publius Wilson.

Charles Dickson retired after fourteen years as Assistant Registrar at Georgia Tech. He attended Atlanta Boys' High School and Emory University. After service in the Coast Guard during the Korean War, he attended graduate school at Emory and Georgia Tech. He and his wife live in Dunwoody, Georgia, and visit elderly relatives.

Launches from a Paper World

Priscilla Carr

At the Charles Bulfinch Elementary School in the Mission Hill section of Boston in the 1950s, every teacher I had from kindergarten through grade six was, of course, Irish, and what we termed an "old maid." My pudgy, plain, and single sixth-grade teacher, Miss Cotter, wore her hair knotted on top of her head and consistently dressed in a dark-blue suit and sensible pumps, and, to many in my neighborhood, appeared to be one those unfortunate women.

Her sixth-grade students, however, saw it differently. Under her tutelage, a room full of wide-eyed eleven-year-olds used papier-mâché to replicate our planet. She helped us comprehend that the world beyond our narrow borders was multidimensional and fascinating. How? We built cardboard volcanoes and whittled canyons. We glued paper grass to recreate Argentine pampas, and even erected an aluminum-foil Eiffel Tower, all of which we gingerly placed on the seven continents we created. As we shaped our paper planet, we explored the history and customs of its countries and cultures and often smelled, tasted, and digested international foods we prepared on a small burner to accompany the lesson.

I had fallen a bit in love with Miss Cotter, and it unsettled me when my mother and Gran and their gossiping friends clucked "tsk tsk" when they mentioned her name, as if they were privy to something shameful about her. Even when I wandered off to toss my ball or jump rope, I attuned my ears to the clucking group, and thus heard Mrs. O'Leary when she sighed and bemoaned Miss Cotter's fate. "Such a wasted life for a woman."

They lamented the fact Miss Cotter didn't have children and somewhat sympathetically summed up her destiny as "a born mother who will never know the joys. . . ." The more I heard, the more I was convinced they couldn't be talking about the same Miss Cotter. *Our* Miss Cotter had dozens of children and loved us all and was very joyous.

Gran had the final word that day. "Poor woman. Every night she eats alone."

Miss Cotter did not dine alone. She regularly showed us pictures of her eating with international friends who were dressed in colorful robes, shawls, ponchos, and hats. She brought us samples of intriguing dishes such as Spanish paella, a Greek eggplant casserole called moussaka, and a steamy, puffy sweet bread called naan from Nepal. Unlike our mothers, she cooked with olive oil, and she took the time to explain how to create and use a marinade.

Still, the women whispered and shook their heads. My mother would drag her hands across her lap and sputter, "And what kind of an example is Miss Cotter setting for our girls with such high falutin' cooking? And on a teacher's salary." I couldn't understand why the exciting and fascinating things Miss Cotter did always upset them.

I loved looking at pictures of Miss Cotter's adventures and was particularly intrigued by one of her posing in front of a large green tent. She was dressed in khaki shorts with a matching khaki jacket, and a big, domed hat that must have been crushing her bun. When I asked why she was wearing Boy Scout clothes, she explained it was a safari suit. Later that night, I looked up the definition of *safari* and easily envisioned Miss Cotter crossing the Kenyan landscape in a jeep. I could almost see the amazed look on her round face when she saw lions and elephants and zebras up close. I was so impressed by her courage. I asked an endless stream of questions about the safari. Her stories enthralled me, but when I described the outfit to Gran, before she listened to another word, she sniffed, "With those thighs and that rear end, she wears shorts and has someone take a picture of her? May the saints preserve us! How on earth was she brought up?"

Our beloved Miss Cotter got into more trouble than anyone I knew, particularly when she skipped Mass on Sunday mornings to go on cruises to Rhode Island and Cape Cod, which was just not done in our neighborhood, and *really* set those tongues to clucking. The usual crowd perched on the front steps and quickly made it clear where they thought Miss Cotter's soul would go if her cruise ship sank or her plane crashed. And I, susceptible to the power of their words, immediately pictured her cruise ship sinking straight down to hell.

They found it scandalous that she traveled "unaccompanied." But the elders decided it was all right if she took such risks with her life. "She doesn't have a husband or children," Mrs. Maloney quipped, shrugging her shoulders, "so . . . no one would be without a wife or a mother."

I was still gasping when Widow Rooney mockingly said, "Who *would* miss her, that silly cat?" Astonishingly, they all laughed and slapped their thighs!

"God only knows if she's going to confession or Mass in those foreign countries," said Mrs. Maloney, the leader of this makeshift Irish council and final word on all matters of importance, and then made an alarming proclamation. "If she crashes or sinks, it will serve her right."

"It will be her own fault if she gets kidnapped or murdered," agreed Mrs. O'Neill, nodding her head.

But Widow Rooney had one more scathing remark. "*That* would put the fear of God into our girls."

I felt stunned and confused. How could the loss of this dynamic, vibrant, and amazing woman not matter to anyone? What about me! What about all of us kids? I ran to my room to cry, and later dreamt of planes crashing and ships sinking.

But, thankfully, she didn't die. In fact, Miss Cotter selected me as her academic assistant and let me help her correct papers during lunch, especially our spelling and vocabulary tests. When we took breaks from that task, she would show me a page from her travel log. One day she showed me a picture of her on a camel under which she had scribbled, "Took camel to Pyramids. Suffocating heat." Because I was again mesmerized, she loaned me a book on the construction of pyramids. Later I convinced Mary Martha Hurley and Kevin Mark Riley to help me construct some on our three-dimensional, papier-mâché world.

I also looked up *suffocation* and when I questioned the literal use of that word the next day, Miss Cotter explained she used a "writer's liberty" in her description. "You're a budding writer. Yes, indeed. One day you'll keep a travel log. Oh, yes, Priscilla, you'll see this big, bold, beautiful world, and you will speak some of its languages, too." There was no doubt in her mind. "Some people live in their living rooms, and others, like you, dear girl, live in the wide, wide world."

Later, I thought about her outstretched arms and wondered just how wide the earth really was, so I looked it up. Miss Cotter was so pleased she gifted me with *Information Please* and the *World Almanac* for Christmas. That summer she dropped off a set of *Encyclopedia Britannica* and a bundle of hardcover children's classics. My mother and Gran sniffed disapprovingly at the time, but I loved those books—each and every one of them.

We moved to New Hampshire that summer, and I never had an opportunity to see Miss Cotter again. But all these years later, I have never forgotten her or her individualism, her enthusiasm, and her stimulating teaching style. In later years, as someone who also became a teacher, I often marveled at how many of my classmates believed he or she was Miss Cotter's favorite. At the Charles Bullfinch School in 1956, Miss Cotter introduced and accompanied a room full of enchanted eleven-year-olds to each continent and left each one of us perceiving that she or he was the center of her world. Imagine that!

Priscilla Carr began pursuing a new career as a multilingual poet, memoirist, essayist, and freelance journalist five years ago. She and her husband travel throughout the world utilizing educational home-stays and Elderhostel programs so they can be amongst the natives, speaking the language, soaking up the culture, and enjoying the cuisine.

Abandoned in Boston

Bonnie Burns

I attended elementary school in the early 1950s in a small town in Massachusetts, right in the heart of Middlesex County. As a little kid, it never sunk in where I lived, and my parents never took us to visit "those tourist spots," so I just romped through childhood, played on the banks of a river traveled by Thoreau, passed many a historic colonial house on the way to school, and was completely oblivious to the rusting canal locks on the edge of town where the oldest canal in the country once existed.

And then I had the good fortune to have Miss Davis as my seventh-grade homeroom teacher. Miss Davis was a slight lady with straight dark graying hair cut just below her ears and long bangs that reached the tip of her eyebrows. Her hair was always the same length, as if she trimmed it each week. Miss

Davis was also a very neat person who dressed in simple, tailored clothing. Her sensible, highly polished shoes clicked officiously when she walked into the room. The only frivolous item she allowed herself were brightly colored ties or a silk ascot at the neck of her blouse. She rarely wore the same one twice.

Seventh grade is an awkward, transitional age, so there were many adolescent dramas and noisy antics, especially at the end of a long school day. But Miss Davis was, after so many years of teaching, impervious to our chaos. She closed the hallway door and walked slowly to her desk, heels clicking on the wood floor. Then she calmly looked at the wall clock and scanned the room, waiting for us to become quiet. As we settled down, she picked up a book off the desk, opened it slowly, and began to read out loud to us.

Week after week, before she uttered the first word, the classroom was quiet, hungrily awaiting the next installment of *Johnny Tremain,* the classic story of a youth who participated in the Revolutionary War. It had mystery, action, suspense, and the hero was someone our own age. The story was alive with real people that until then had been only names in dull textbooks. The prim Miss Davis read with a dramatic flair that surprised us at first, but then we looked forward to her enactments. She always stopped a little bit short of the last bell so we could discuss the day's reading. I soon wanted to learn more of New England and the Revolutionary War, so I eagerly tackled extra reading assignments.

Toward the end of the school year Miss Davis announced that she had planned a surprise field trip for us. We would take a charter bus to see the locales where the events of the book took place. I was thrilled! Not only was it my first field trip, but we would also be visiting the very places I had been reading about for months. The big day came and our homeroom class boarded the big tour bus—a real bus, not a yellow school bus that would label us as schoolchildren. We were real tourists on a day-long adventure. Miss Davis took roll call as usual and then sat in the front seat, chatting with the bus driver while we students bounced around in the back, taking in the sights along the road, exchanging the contents of our sack lunches.

When we arrived in Boston, we met up with our tour guide at Paul Revere's house. Excited to see the house, we stood to disembark, but the guide claimed he was only hired to point out the sites, not babysit a bunch of school kids. Dismayed, we all stared as he angrily left the bus and stalked off down the street. Was our day to end here? What about Johnny Tremain? What about the Old North Church? Minutemen and Redcoats, spies, and midnight rides?

Miss Davis ran her hand through her hair, which left a few strands sticking out. She set her lips and turned to the bus driver. We all sat down and waited quietly, for we had never seen her muss her hair. She asked the driver a few questions and we heard him reply that yes, he knew all the stops and figured between the two of them, they knew more than that tour guide anyway. We cheered as he announced that the first stop was indeed, Paul Revere's house.

Miss Davis had prepared notes from the book to illustrate each stop and we gathered to listen to her first recitation. Here is where we identified with Johnny Tremain's apprenticeship to a silversmith. This was our first illustration, our first peek into the book and history. We gazed on the craftsmanship and beauty of silver, awed by the sleek silver bowls and intricate designs on cups and tableware. We came to know Paul Revere as a man and a patriot.

The bus drove on through Boston to the harbor, past monuments and landmarks, while we listened to Miss Davis's descriptions and then her account of the Boston Tea Party. We boarded the USS *Constitution*, the ship popularly known as "Old Ironsides." How small it seemed next to the modern battleships moored in the harbor, but how great it was to stand on her wooden decks under the great masts, and each of us had to ring the ship's bell more than once.

We sat quietly in the pews of the Old North Church and imagined the lamps lit so long ago in the belfry; "One if by land, two if by sea," whispered Miss Davis, pointing upward.

With youthful vigor, we climbed the winding stairs of the Bunker Hill Monument—twice. When we returned, breathless, Miss Davis informed us that the first Minuteman to die at the Battle of Bunker Hill, Asa Pollard, was from our hometown of Billerica. We gasped in horror when we learned a British cannonball fired from way out in the harbor had beheaded him!

The last and best stop of the day was the countryside and battlefields of Concord and Lexington. Running past the Minuteman statue, over the bridge where the shot "heard round the world" was fired, I learned that our own Concord River flowed beneath us. Here was where it all began. This is where the Minutemen gathered, ready to meet the Redcoats on the march to Concord. This is where Johnny Tremain's friend, Rab, was injured and later died, after his first battle.

As we headed home, I know that in spite of ourselves, in spite of our antics and youthful enthusiasm, we all gained a new perspective and appreciation of our countryside, its history and literature.

Many years later I returned as an adult and revisited the same historical venues, this time slowly strolling, instead of running, across the bridge at Concord and Lexington. I thought of and thanked Miss Davis, who taught me so much of literature and history and how the two worked so well together, just as they did when a teacher and a bus driver from Boston saved the day.

Bonnie Burns now resides in the High Desert of Central Oregon but still pines for New England's autumn foliage. She travels often and spends her free time on her first loves: reading and writing. Her work has appeared in *Reader's Digest*, *Random Acts of Kindness*, and *Green Prints* magazine.

Practical Physics

Dennis C. Bentley

I had made a grievous mistake. I could tell the very moment I walked into the classroom and spotted the top ten scholastic seniors at their desks. Something was very, very wrong.

The class I had actually signed up for was full, and I had arrived late to the rescheduling party. Unfortunately, I needed a science credit to graduate, and my options were severely limited. Physical science, biology, and chemistry were pretty much the domain of freshman and sophomores. So I chose physics because I thought it would save the day. The counselor reassured me that it dealt with energy, and electrons, and simple machines. She didn't mention the advanced mathematics.

I had barely squeaked by in math classes; my algebra and geometry grades had been gifts.

Because I wasn't a noisy or bothersome student, my algebra and geometry teachers had essentially awarded me a score of seventy—a very low, but passing grade—by charitably rounding up the prevailing failing scores. From all appearances, I just didn't have the type of brainpower required to understand math concepts that employed a string of complex letters and numbers. A reality that presented problems as $A = C - D + X$ where $X = $ Pi and D is a non-prime integer—whatever that means—simply wasn't part of my reality.

When I bolted from the room and dashed to the counselor's office, I was coldly informed that there was no way out. There were no other classes I could take and graduate on time. And time was a critical factor. I had plans, big ones that I had decided on two years prior. I was going to join the air force and study electronics. I really never desired anything else. When I decided on that option, it felt so right I was ready to go as soon as my senior year was behind me.

Alas, I now found myself in physics, where almost immediately, the complex math talk started. My teacher, Mr. Bowen, was a nice enough man, hardly intellectually threatening as his large frame and round features would fit a bus driver, or professional bowler, but his lectures became long discourses about joules, ergs, thermodynamics, and other freakishly complex concepts that just were not on my ruler. I barely learned to use a slip-stick (pretentious slang for the slide rule) to invent bizarre and seemingly ridiculous answers to impossibly complex problems.

The pure math quizzes looked as if they were derived from a crazed, demon-possessed, random number shredder that vomited numbers onto a page and asked me to find an impossibly disguised missing link. Without really understanding how I arrived at the answer, and no idea if they were anywhere in the ballpark, I scribbled them onto my homework page or quiz and hoped for the best. I not only failed the quizzes; I scored sub-atomic level, mass-less, volume-less failing grades. Within weeks, I adopted a "Why bother?" attitude.

Mr. Bowen certainly saw me struggle—it would've been difficult to ignore—and although he seemed sympathetic, I don't think he knew what to do about it. In all likelihood, he was as skeptical as I that I would ever conquer the math skills needed to comprehend physics. At best, I moved at a crippled snail's pace, which drove his pride and joy—those annoying, certified, scholastic *mathletes*—bonkers.

Since volunteering to help the teachers with housekeeping chores had boosted my previous math grades, I stayed after class often. I was erasing indecipherable scripts and formulas from the chalkboard when I told him about my goal to study electronics in the Air Force. Although he arched an eyebrow, he seemed impressed. "Are you sure about this?" he asked.

"I'm quite good at electronics," I explained, cheered by his newfound interest. "I've been wiring lights, radios, speakers, amplifiers, tape recorders, and record players for years. I recently built a fully functional radio station with parts of vacuum tube amps, walkie-talkies, my father's reel-to-reel tape recorder, and whatever else I could find or pilfer."

"Mr. Bentley," he said, smiling. "Do you have more time after classes?"

"I almost always stay late. I have to ride home with my mother, the English teacher."

"I have an idea," he said, scratching the top of his head where an unruly comb-over wasn't really hiding the spot where thinning brown hair once resided.

For the rest of the school year, after everyone had gone for the day, I met Mr. Bowen in the science lab. We wired up magnets, lights, generators, and any scrap we could find. We scoured the classrooms and labs for dusty, unused, and neglected equipment, and then used our noggins to find ingenious ways to use them. We fired up an old and horribly inaccurate voltmeter and took measurements, pausing to change pieces or to turn big grey knobs and record the variances. We pushed it so far one day that the cranky, old voltmeter caught fire, leaving a trail of stink and blue smoke. Luckily, Mr. Bowen had been at the helm, and he merely shrugged, put out the fire, and suggested we keep going.

We never discussed ergs or joules. Instead, we focused on what happened to a magnetic field if we wrapped it with aluminum foil or dipped it into a steel can. We tried wacky experiments, like trying to listen to a radio in a small vacuum chamber, measuring magnetic fields with what looked like a stainless-steel fishing scale, or touching things to see how much hotter they got as voltage increased (answer: *a lot!*). Everything we did felt like child's play, but also somewhat dangerous, rebellious, hands-on fun. When someone approached, we would crouch down to avoid discovery. I don't know how much I actually learned about classic academic physics, but at the end of the semester, Mr. Bowen gifted me with a passing grade—seventy, like always—enough for me to graduate on time.

Not only did I make it to the Air Force, but within eighteen months I graduated from a thirty-six-week electronic communications curriculum, and, at the youthful age of nineteen, was selected to be an instructor of electronics at Sheppard Air Force Base in Texas. I finally understood the Pythagorean theorem, and how to use it to calculate the capacitive reactance in AC circuits. I knew it so well, I was teaching it to others—patiently.

Just to give him a laugh, I wrote Mr. Bowen a letter telling him how his hard work had paid off and explaining, in great technical detail, why that old voltmeter had fried.

Dennis C. Bentley earned a BS in Occupational Education from Wayland Baptist College, Plainview, Texas. He applied his practical electronics knowledge and skills to carve out a career in commercial audio manufacturing, and finally, maintaining large computer systems. He is currently an information technology consultant in St. Louis.

The Days of Bloom

Sande Boritz Berger

He would have loved that I Googled him, and loved, even more, the sound of the twenty-first-century search-engine phrase. Professor Harry Bloom stressed the importance of choosing just the right word, and not solely for its meaning; he relished the uniqueness a properly chosen word lent to a phrase.

When I entered his classroom in 1963, Professor Bloom was already a legend. He was known to be an extremely demanding taskmaster who held the highest expectations. You couldn't skate work by Professor Bloom—lackluster attempts to write poetry and prose were returned with a resounding slap of paper on the desk and acerbic criticism scrawled around the manuscript's edges. He expected his students to bleed on the page.

Even though others had forewarned me of his intimidating presence, I saw him as a sweet old man—though he was probably around fifty at the time! As a child, I was obsessed with the story of Heidi and her heroic grandfather—an embodiment of someone who would shield a young girl from danger and find her if she was lost. Instead of fearing Professor Bloom, I spent my time fervently hoping that he would find me—the real *me,* hidden under a cloak of social propriety. I pictured him as a long-lost relative who had returned home with instructive stories to tell. In my eyes, he became a fascinating blend of scholar, elf, and rabbi. I loved imagining him alternately working late into the night, honing his novel, and solemnly hunched over an ancient copy of the Talmud reading by candlelight.

I walked into that first creative writing class quaking with giddy excitement, praying, of course, that it didn't show. Although I dressed for the occasion in my finest ribbed turtleneck and matching pleated skirt, I was focused, like most of the student body, on being one hour away from dashing downtown to Jerry's Bar and Grill, where, if lucky, I'd meet the boy of my dreams—dreams that quickly disintegrated after one awful or awkward Saturday-night date.

Even though he was well aware that we were antsy, waiting for our weekend to commence, or perhaps most assuredly because he knew that about us, Professor Bloom adopted a painfully slow, almost Southern drawl paired with facial gestures and body movements that resembled spastic mime. For the rest of the class, he spoke very little, but he stared so intently I felt as if his eyes burrowed into my soul. I squirmed until splinters nibbled through the fabric of my skirt and pierced my behind.

On that day and on every day afterwards, I watched with juvenile fascination as he carefully packed tobacco in his pipe, pressed it down at least ten times, and then repeatedly chewed the stem without ever once lighting it. Still, the redolence of cherry tobacco wafted through the air. And that smell, coupled with the sound of hissing radiators, provided the sensual sound track of Professor Bloom's creative-writing diatribes. When he read passages he loved, Professor Bloom lowered his pale, hooded eyes and read them aloud, slowly, reverently, while occasionally and unexpectedly peering upward over his metal bifocals to see if we were listening intently. No matter what he read, his love for the resonance in words—the mystery found in language—was infectious. He often paused to repeat a line and always ended each reading with a smile.

And then he would abruptly turn and face the class like an inquisitor. "What does that mean to you, Miss B?" he might say, startling me, tossing ice water on the sweet, mellow thoughts swirling around my brain. "Just . . . to you," he added, pointing to me, watching my face deepen to a russet hue.

Sometimes I attempted an answer, but my thoughts would feel censored, my voice utterly foreign. I sounded like a wounded sparrow, not the intelligent, discerning, budding writer that I wanted to project. After a few deadly seconds of enduring my fragmented replies, he would mercifully move on, albeit not without a glance backward that clearly said, "Work on it, Miss B." And later, I would revisit the story or poem hoping to decipher the deeper, truer meaning that Professor Bloom had wanted me to grasp.

On those spring afternoons, no matter what he read, he read it with undisguised enthusiasm. Sometimes he read "the tawdry, terrible poems" of Robinson Jeffers, the "unforgettable images in words" by Marianne Moore, or the "stream-of-consciousness" of Emily Dickinson. He wanted us to learn from the mistakes and to emulate the success of other writers. He did what any great teacher would do—he taught us to read with our eyes and our souls. He taught us to judge for ourselves and to open to our own mystery. He taught us to have high standards and to reach deeper for just the right word, or just the right feeling.

As a child, when I felt inspired, I used to scribble words on the flowered wallpaper in my attic room. When I felt inspired in college, I scratched poetry on the inside of matchbook covers from Jerry's Bar or on napkins while drinking black coffee in the campus' dungeon-like coffee shop. When Professor Bloom saw one of my "masterpieces" lying on my desk, I quickly offered to rewrite the poem before handing it in. "Don't you dare," he bellowed. "I want your poem without the dressings; I want it regurgitated and as raw as it was meant to be; I want it hot off the press while it's still *your* poem."

Halfway through the semester, we began reading fiction. Professor Bloom loved the sparseness of prose, the need to hit the reader head-on, and the requirement to make every single word count in short-short stories. He drilled the form into our brain—a short-short story must have a beginning, a middle, and an end that delivered quickly. The form required a masterful hand that could quickly and proficiently infuse the stories with form, structure, feeling, and finality.

One week after we'd handed in our stories, Professor Bloom strode into the class surveying us as if he were seeing our eager faces for the first time. He created so much tension with his gaze, I felt I had to move, do something, jump, or I might scream. I couldn't just let him stare me down. I had poured my heart and soul into my story. All those secrets I had guarded for so long now rested in Professor Bloom's hands. Now he knew everything. He could literally see through me, down to the soft marrow of my bones. I had bled for Harry Bloom, and I was terrified of what he would say. Would he crush my spirit? I shifted my gaze toward the window and focused on the valley below.

When I heard his chair scrape against the slanted oak floor and looked up to see his lips forming words, my ears blocked out the hissing of the radiator and the mumbling students all around me. What I heard was, "This, my dear students, is a genuine, masterfully written short story." Without a single glance in my direction, he began slowly reading my words, validating my worth as a writer and a woman with stories to tell by reading it with reverence and wisdom and grace. He not only gifted me with more hope than I had ever known, he instilled me with courage and fostered not only an unrelenting drive to write, but a sense of duty to write from my heart and soul—over and over again, on that day, and all the days to follow.

Sande Boritz Berger has been published in many best-selling anthologies, including the *Cup of Comfort* series, and literary reviews such as *Confrontation*, *TriQuarterly Magazine*, and *The Southampton Review*. She is currently finishing a MFA in writing and literature at Stony Brook Southampton College and has completed her first novel.

Finally in Tune with the Band Director

Judy Gerlach

Labor Day weekend had come to a close, marking the end of summer fun and the beginning of a new chapter in my school career—the junior high years, those long-awaited and much-anticipated years of transition from child to teen. I vividly remember the walk from the main educational building to the music building on the first day of classes. Scattered autumn leaves rustled beneath my shoes as my girlfriends and I made our way across the walkway to the building that would be home to our band class for the next three years.

My heart quickened as I stared down at my flute case. My knuckles had whitened from clenching the handle. "I don't want to be in band any more," I told my friends.

"I heard that the band director is really demanding," Beth chimed in. She wore a smirk on her face. I laughed in spite of myself when I noticed her tight grip on her clarinet case.

Standing in the lobby of the music building, I took a deep breath before starting up the stairs to the band room. I was just beginning to feel confident about going into that class when three eighth-grade boys barged their way past us.

"Better not be late to band class, babies! Mr. McCoy will lecture you in front of everyone," one taunted. Although we picked up our pace, I seriously considered an about-face.

My confidence sufficiently shaken, I meandered my way around the first semicircle of chairs to the second row, assuming the first row was reserved for the eighth- and ninth-grade flutists. Wrong. There were plenty of chairs for all of us in the front row. I sat down next to my friend Pat. I glanced back at Beth in the third row and suddenly wished I'd chosen to play the clarinet instead.

I'd heard from some of the older students that Mr. McCoy loved to lecture. They were right. We didn't play our instruments much that first day. As if he could read my mind, he talked about how important it was to stay in the band. "You picked out an instrument. You learned to play it. You've practiced diligently, and now you're in junior high. Now that you've come this far, the last thing you want to do is be a quitter."

Fair enough. I'd grown up with the "finish what you've started" principle. By the end of that first class, I knew I was in the band for the long haul.

I'd also heard talk of Mr. McCoy's "brutal" teaching tactics. It was true. He was such a perfectionist. Very intimidating.

Very strict. If a musical violation occurred during a practice, he'd actually stop the whole band to point out the transgression. His ability to hone in on the source never ceased to amaze me. But, horror of horrors, he didn't stop there. He actually took the time to work with each student individually to correct the mistake. From properly positioning one's lips to holding the instrument correctly, he was right there. One on one. Right in front of everyone! How humiliating. Some kids didn't like it, but they didn't quit.

I adapted easily enough to this aspect of Mr. McCoy's class. I was used to having parents at home watching over everything that I did, making sure I did it right. Or die trying!

Mr. McCoy showed a lot of compassion for the less fortunate, too. There was a boy who had come to him with a crippled foot and hand wondering if there was anything he could do to be a part of the band. In a very short time, to everyone's amazement, this band director had taught the boy how to hold a mallet in his crippled hand so that he could learn to play the marimba. Mr. McCoy could tell when someone had a heart for something. Attitude was important.

Then came that fateful day when Mr. McCoy singled me out for one of his visual aid demonstrations. It happened following a musical infraction in which nearly the entire band had failed to hold out the last two whole notes of a phrase for their written value of eight beats, running out of breath after only six beats. "No-o-o!" he thundered. "Seven! Eight!" He pounded his fist on his music stand two times for effect. "Breathe from the diaphragm!" Next thing I knew, he'd pulled up a chair in front of everyone and called me up to demonstrate an exercise in diaphragmatic breathing. For those of us who didn't know where or what a diaphragm was, this exercise was designed to help us feel the air fill up in our diaphragms.

"Judy, I want you to sit right here." I sat in the chair, refusing to make eye contact with anyone, but I couldn't keep from hearing the chuckles. "Now, lean forward until your head touches your knees." I did, and a stern look from Mr. McCoy at my audience checked any further revelry. With his hand on my back, he continued, "Stay in that position and draw in as much air as you can." Amazing! It worked. But, in spite of the fact that the whole band had to do the same exercise next, I felt mortified at being singled out and asked to demonstrate how to bend way, way over in front of my classmates.

I crept into the hallway expecting ridicule, and when those three aforementioned older boys followed me to my next class laughing and singing, "Teacher's pet, teacher's pet," it was all I could take. I cried to my mom about it later, but she said I couldn't quit over something like that. Luckily, it was a one-time exposure; Mr. McCoy didn't single me out any more. I liked it better that way, and we got along fine. I was glad I wasn't a quitter.

Thanks to Mr. McCoy, we became first-rate musicians and could play music well beyond our age level with award-winning results. Strict, intimidating, a demanding perfectionist, methodical, caring—Mr. McCoy was willing to go the extra mile. He had all the hallmarks of an excellent teacher, but still I felt relieved when I moved on to the high school band.

When this infamous band director passed away, I was blown away by the deluge of e-mails and letters spilling over with accolades that poured in from all over the country. Many were read at his funeral. The man had made an indelible impression on countless numbers of students, who admitted employing his methods and principles in one way or another regardless of their chosen profession. The teacher whom I'd considered the bane of my junior high years, the formidable Mr. McCoy, was a real hero after all. I'd been in tune with that idea all along. As story after story was read, I sobbed away, alongside a sizable representation of students who'd traveled long distances to be there. The crippled student, now a man in his fifties, also showed up. Ironically, as life would have it, he was one of the few who'd followed through with a career as a professional musician!

But for me, this whole scene was more personal.

You see, Mr. McCoy wasn't just my band director. He was my dad.

His legacy speaks for itself. I wish I'd told him before it was too late that he was the best teacher I ever had.

Judy Gerlach works as a personal assistant for her husband Greg's video production company in Lexington, Kentucky. A published author of church drama, she began her writing career writing plays and sketches for her church. Judy has written numerous short stories and two novels. She still enjoys playing the flute.

The World's Worst Dresser

Glenn Hameroff

Dr. Hugh Cleland wore clothing that clashed with itself and with all standards of reasonable dress. In my mind's eye, I can still see him dressed in his black tweed hat, multicolored iridescent sports jacket, and blue plaid trousers. Coke-bottle eyeglasses and a particularly high-pitched voice accompanied his unique style of dressing. He not only seemed colorblind, he had no sense of patterning, or texture, or appropriateness. He frequently paired plaids with stripes, and favored a ratty wool sweater, replete with moth holes and pilling—in the dead heat of summer. His appearance as he entered the classroom quieted students down immediately.

When he spoke, however, Dr. Cleland not only mesmerized his students, he gained tremendous respect within the university community because he successfully breached university standards as easily as he breached fashion standards. Quite simply, Dr. Cleland went far beyond the call of duty in providing his students with a wealth of information and a hunger for a wider perspective than the ones usually gained from more traditional teachers. Unlike most teachers of his day, Dr. Cleland never steered clear of controversy; he not only encouraged, he absolutely championed independent thinking.

Not only was he unique in terms of dress, decorum, speech, and the desire to teach students how to think rather than how to memorize rote facts, Dr. Cleland was a democratic socialist who didn't feel the need to temper his principles—or his speech—to comply with superfluous social values or ways of discussing or defining politics. Because he had been a staunch supporter of the progressive labor movement and had spent most of his early years speaking up for, and fighting for, the rights of the people—as opposed to those of our government, or big business, or the wealthy—Dr. Cleland believed in and held firm to his principles, even when being a socialist took on another meaning and turned off his colleagues or casual listeners at cocktail parties. Unlike many, who strove to always appear "politically correct," Dr. Cleland never cowered in the presence of ignorance. To his dying day, he remained a democratic socialist and continued to express his opinions in an increasingly conservative university setting, as well as when participating in political rallies or social events.

I always felt blessed that I was one of Dr. Cleland's students in the 1960s, a heyday in political discourse. It was a time when politics and freedom were on the front burner; a time when antiquated teaching methods simply no longer fit; a time when rebellious students took their faculty and university administrators to task, demanding a broadened and more liberal curriculum. Dr. Cleland, of course, was ahead of the curve, and his American history course at Stony Brook University became wildly popular.

Dr. Cleland's Socratic forum both engaged and fired up his students who lined up to register in his classes and quickly adopted his questioning approach in social settings. His instructional mantra—"How do you know that?"—resounded in the hallways and cafeterias, becoming our way of reordering our perceptions and thinking for ourselves. The tone of his questions and his enthusiastic receptivity always invited students to participate. Dr. Cleland was an amusing, enlightening Socratic gadfly whose lust for enthusiastic curiosity definitely inspired me to become a better student—and, eventually, a better teacher.

When I graduated from Stony Brook, I landed a job as a social studies teacher. Even if the 1960s had toppled academic steeples at the university level, local high schools remained staunchly conservative and rooted to their tried-and-true course structures and teaching methods. Before I had any license, or dared to experiment with new teaching ideas in elective courses, I had to earn tenure. Once that was achieved, I drew upon everything I had learned from Dr. Cleland and created a class entitled "Great Moral Issues" that combined controversial ethics with a speaker component. Each student was required to obtain a speaker and to conduct a seminar based on that speaker's particular ethical stance. Some school district officials and parents bristled, but—in the same way that I had done under Dr. Cleland's tutelage—the students responded very favorably.

When I asked Dr. Cleland to come in and speak, he was delighted and, over the course of the next twenty years, came in at least once a year, and often five or six times. His fashion sense remained quirky at best, but his enthusiasm for teaching never waned. He loved provoking thought. As soon as he stood before a roomful of eager faces, everyone recognized him as a masterful teacher who took great joy in communicating with students. Once the students looked past his mismatching socks and outdated wide-leg trousers, they, too, fell under his magical spell. In all my days of teaching, I have never come upon anyone better.

Glenn Hameroff was a high-school history teacher until the advance of Parkinson's disease cut his career short. His writing provides a creative outlet, and he felt inspired to write this about his former professor because he firmly believes "We really need more heroes today."

Learning to Fly

Susan B. Townsend

One Friday afternoon, just before the final bell, my tenth-grade science teacher, Mr. Humphrey, called my name. I froze. What had I done? Was he angry? Did he know, somehow, that I hadn't been paying attention for at least the last half hour?

His eyes looked kind. "Can I see you for a minute after class?" He asked this loudly enough for all to hear. I felt a fire of humiliation and jerked my head once in agreement. The murmurs and snickers made it clear; once again, I provided entertainment for the masses.

When the bell rang, my classmates scurried away, laughing and talking. On Fridays, the air turned festive as good-natured teasing and tentative plans were called out. I, of course, did not partake in the teasing and was rarely the recipient of any invitations.

"You have to make an effort," my mother scolded me. "When you're new, you have to work at making friends." I wondered then if she had a manual of phrases for every miserable occasion in the life of a child who just didn't fit in. There was something broken in me, I decided. Always had been. Always would be.

Mr. Humphrey beckoned me to the front of the class. "Wait here. I'll be right back," he said, and then disappeared into the storage room. He returned carrying a small wire cage and placed it on the counter. I stared at the tiny sparrow huddled in the corner, one wing tucked neatly against his body, the other drooping as if glued to his side.

"I rescued him from the jaws of my cats," he said. "I think his wing is broken. It can be quite perilous, you know."

What I knew was that Mr. Humphrey heard the cruel words directed my way and undoubtedly had seen me bite my lip and blink back tears. He watched me sit alone, with my head down, as the others selected their lab partners. Was this his way of telling me that I could fix whatever was wrong? Perhaps, like my mother, he believed that my situation was temporary—that one day I would wake up special and sought after. "Do you think you can help me out?" he asked.

I stared at the periodic table of the elements hanging under the clock and said nothing. I wanted to flash a radiant smile a lá Kelly Watson, popular and charismatic head cheerleader, and cheerily reply, "You bet! I know exactly what to do." But I didn't have a clue. Me fixing that bird's wing would be like a boy asking me to next week's dance—both were in the realm of never going to happen. I shook my head, and shrugged my shoulders. "Sorry."

He sighed. "I was hoping we could save him." I shot him a quick glance and saw him smile. "My wife is always telling me I'm too soft-hearted, and maybe she's right, but it would be cruel to let this innocent little sparrow suffer."

My heart began to pound. What did he mean? Was he going to kill it? I put my hand on the cage. "No," I said, looking straight into my teacher's eyes. "We've got to try to save him." Abruptly aroused from his lethargy, the bird panicked, fluttering and throwing himself against the wire. I took my sweater out of my book bag and placed it over the cage, and the little sparrow quieted down.

Mr. Humphrey's eyes widened. "Looks like you've had some experience."

"My parakeet likes to be covered at night and when he freaks out. That's all I really know about birds." Neither of us spoke for several long seconds. "If you had a Popsicle stick and some adhesive tape, we could make a splint."

I waited for Mr. Humphrey to laugh or to tell me in his quiet, gentle voice that he didn't think my idea would work. But he looked thoughtful, disappeared again into the storage room, and returned with a stick, tape, and gloves. "You've got little hands," he said, " and I'm afraid I'd squash the poor thing. So if you'll hold him, I think I can tape his wing into place."

The sparrow trembled so hard I could feel his heart beating against my skin. I was terrified he would die. Luckily, Mr. Humphrey managed to reposition the bird's wing and secure it with the makeshift splint. I put the sparrow into the cage, and Mr. Humphrey draped the sweater over it. "You don't mind watching over him, do you? You can put a dish of water in his cage when you get home, and he'd probably eat parakeet seed."

I nodded. "I think I'll leave his cover on for a couple of days to make sure he stays quiet."

"You're very kind," Mr. Humphrey said. "I knew you'd have a knack for this kind of thing."

The bird chirped the whole way home, and any temporary feelings of elation faded and my normal sense of dread returned. By the time I reached my house, I was angry with Mr. Humphrey—and myself—for thinking that we could fix this little bird, that if I nurtured him, he might be able to fly again.

As soon as I reached home, I removed the sweater to peer at him, and he resumed his wild and terrified dance. I tapped the cage to make him stop, and he paused for a moment and looked at me. "Why does everyone think broken wings can be fixed?" I whispered.

I covered the cage and took it up to my room, filled a mayonnaise jar lid with water, and put it in the cage. Since he wasn't used to eating from a cup like my parakeet, I sprinkled parakeet seed on the cage floor.

The next morning when I lifted the covering, I felt elated again. The whole seeds I had given him had been reduced to hulls. He had eaten! I had actually done something worthwhile!

On Monday morning, I eagerly updated Mr. Humphrey. My excitement flipped to horror, however, when he proceeded to tell the class about "our wounded sparrow." At that moment, I envied the bird and longed to disappear into my own covered cage, but my classmates surprised me. Although a few snickered, many expressed genuine interest and congratulated me on saving the bird's life.

Over the following weeks, even popular kids asked about the bird. I reported everything, including the scares, like the second time the sparrow tried to lift his injured wing, but it was too soon so I had to clamp it back in place and tape the splint again. The little sparrow was making progress, and while I enjoyed watching him grow frisky and impatient, I worried about that first flight. Maybe I worried that no one would talk to me if I no longer had the bird, or maybe I had fallen in love with his plight.

As if he had read my mind, Mr. Humphrey motioned me over when I was leaving class the next day. "It's been six weeks," he said. "Is our sparrow ready to fly?"

"I guess so," I replied, making no attempt to hide my lack of enthusiasm.

"Hey, I've got a great idea. Why don't you bring the bird to school Friday so we can all watch what happens?"

"Yeah, okay." I turned to scoop up my books. "See you," I said and hurriedly left. Mr. Humphrey remained perched on the edge of his desk, looking concerned and confused.

At home, I stared at the bird. I didn't want to let him go. But when I turned to look at my parakeet, I realized the difference—the parakeet had always lived in a cage, but the sparrow was born to fly. He would feel imprisoned, condemned to a life surrounded by wires.

That Friday, the entire class gathered at the edge of a field behind the school. We all watched silently as Mr. Humphrey carefully removed the splint. When the sparrow flexed his wing, Mr. Humphrey looked over at me with a question in his eyes.

I felt my eyes burn and was afraid I would cry if I tried to speak so I forced a quick nod, and Mr. Humphrey opened his hands. The sparrow stood poised for a moment, and then he took off, both wings flapping. "We have liftoff," Mr. Humphrey announced, and I heard a smattering of applause, followed by cheers.

"Wow," I said and flashed a radiant smile a lá Susan, freshly minted and somewhat famous bird doctor. "Broken wings can be fixed."

Susan B. Townsend, author of *A Bouquet for Mother* and *A Bouquet for Grandmother*, is a writer and stay-at-home mother. She lives on a farm in southeastern Virginia with her husband, five children, and too many animals. She is a contributing editor of *A Cup of Comfort Book of Prayer* and can be reached at *monitor@visi.net*.

Houston, We Have a Problem

Sharyn L. Bolton

The voices of the Mission Control team began the 1993 countdown "Ten . . . nine . . . eight. . . ." And then everyone in the room shouted out the final seven numbers simultaneously. "Solid rocket booster starting liftoff," declared a youthful voice, which caused shrieks of joy audible via intercom from the space shuttle. "Shuttle has left the tower," said another young voice. The room erupted into jubilatory celebration.

Instead of NASA's Kennedy or Johnson Space Center, this Mission Control operated inside a small grade-school library. The controllers, two nine-year-old boys, took their jobs so seriously they completely ignored the excited crowd, consisting of local politicians, news reporters from four Washington State newspapers, parents, thirty students, and an ingenious, exuberant elementary school teacher.

This was no puny reenactment of a real space launch. The clever and industrious Ms. O'Rourke planned and executed the entire extraordinary and quite realistic experience. She meticulously mapped out a rigorous six-month curriculum to help her thirty students (comprised of fourth, fifth, and sixth graders) prepare and execute the mission. By the time their shuttle figuratively got off the ground, the excitement in the room was sufficient to launch a real rocket.

Her vision for the project materialized when the National Science Teachers Association extended her an invitation to attend a two-week program at the NASA Ames Research Center during summer vacation. Ms. O'Rourke returned all fired up and soon fired up the lucky students who were under her charge that fall.

Fortunately, my son Drew was one of those students. From the beginning, he could barely contain his excitement. "Mom, Ms. O'Rourke's going to take us into space!" When I raised an eyebrow, he said, "Not real space, but it's going to be cool. We're going to do everything like real astronauts . . . everything."

Due to her own enthusiasm and desire to offer purposeful learning, Ms. O'Rourke created lesson plans that linked elementary science, math, and rocketry to everything they needed to know to simulate a real shuttle liftoff and complete their mission. With the help of Ms. O'Rourke and his classmates, Drew easily grasped the basic principles of Newton's laws and quickly learned the value of cooperative teamwork.

Ms. O'Rourke helped her students develop and use a computer program that explained the intricacies of the mission and delineated everything they would need to know about space and space travel to complete their "Atlas Mission." By teaching her students how to write a newsletter to spread the word to parents and other classes at the elementary school, Ms. O'Rourke cleverly brought the community together. She also had students write and mail press releases to media outlets and local politicians, and they wrote letters to local businesses asking for financial support.

The students designed the cloth-and-piping mid-deck of the shuttle and, with the help of parent volunteers, built it to fit their specifications. It would house the crew's cockpit and living accommodations for the commander, pilot, medical officer, and three astronauts. They also designed and built a science laboratory to fit in the shuttle.

Ms. O'Rourke enlisted the aid of parents, who quickly became as enthusiastic as their children. One parent wired the school library to serve as mission control and connected it to the classroom that would house the space shuttle. He also provided materials and helped construct the communication system, which combined closed circuit television, computers, and the existing intercom system. Other parents eagerly volunteered to host the event.

As the project progressed, the students underwent rigorous astronaut training, as well as shuttle crew and mission control training. Ms. O'Rourke announced that the students should decide which job matched their goals and skill level, and she then showed them how to prepare a resume that would list and promote their strengths. After all the job applications were completed, she interviewed each child to determine where he or she would best fit.

One afternoon, Drew came bounding in the front door. "Mom! Mom! I'm on Mission Control for the launch!" He proudly showed me his congratulatory letter. "I'm going to be on duty for the blast-off!"

When I read the letter, I was thrilled to see that Ms. O'Rourke missed no opportunity to teach her charges valuable lessons. "It is imperative that you keep your new position in mind as you are no longer just an eminent individual, but a role model for everyone," she wrote. She also clearly delineated Drew's duties as a Mission Control specialist. "You will be contacting the astronauts on your team during the Atlas Mission . . . [and] you will be hosting several area business people and city council members during the launch." Not only was Ms. O'Rourke congratulating Drew on his assignment, she was treating him as if he was already fully capable of achieving his appointed goals and holding him to high expectations.

When it came time to enact the twenty-four-hour simulation of the launch, the children selected as the space crew remained in the shuttle's mid-deck overnight. For realism, these astronauts feasted on freeze-dried army rations and used a portable bathroom brought on board for the duration. Those students serving as Mission Control were also on duty for twenty-four hours so they could be fully prepared for the launch and in constant communication with the shuttle crew.

Once the shuttle was launched, the ground crew focused on completing the mission. Without their knowledge, Ms.

O'Rourke had previously arranged a video conference call with Tom Clausen from the NASA Ames Research Center. At the appointed time, he called. His image appeared on their screen and said, "Houston, we have a problem." He gave them a scenario: The tethered satellite, which the space shuttle crew hoped would successfully survive blastoff and the transit through the Earth's upper atmosphere, was being threatened by an eruption of Mount St. Helens.

Speaking as if addressing a real crew, he said, "So you need to map the volcanic plume and direct the astronauts when to elevate the cable [holding the satellite] and redeploy it." As he outlined the details, the youthful controllers listened intently and then contacted the space shuttle. The students talked back and forth for some time and then bounced ideas off the NASA commander, who helped them come up with a solution. When they had reached a consensus, Commander Clausen coolly said, "It's a go. Proceed with the mission."

I nearly cried as I watched my nine-year-old son smoothly handle the conference call and offer his ideas about how to solve the problem. Later, he kept the same cool head when several local newspaper reporters and city councilmen talked with him about the experience. Because the students had spent six long months amassing information and preparing for this in-depth, imaginative, intensive, hands-on educational project, my son fielded tough questions and handled them with amazing confidence. What parent wouldn't have been extraordinarily proud!

When the shuttle "landed" a full twenty-four hours later, a bedraggled group of students emerged from the mid-deck and joined the student news corps, parents, Mission Control specialists, and Ms. O'Rourke in the school library. We were all exhausted but so thrilled we held our droopy eyes open long enough to celebrate the amazing accomplishment. I had never seen such confident and happy students, inspired to reach for the stars.

Sharyn L. Bolton from Mill Creek, WA, is a proud parent of two adult "perfect children." As a freelance writer, she has been published in local, regional, and national publications. Her credits include essays, short stories, articles, a nonfiction book, and several regional writing awards. She has ghostwritten two nonfiction business books.

All Things Imaginable Are but Nouns
(Jonathan Swift, *Gulliver's Travels*)

Stephen D. Rogers

When it came time for me to prepare for my twenty-fifth high school reunion, I didn't grab my yearbook to review my classmates. Instead, I went to the school's Web site and was thunderstruck when I saw that not one of my teachers was listed among the faculty. I knew that I'd graduated a quarter-century ago, but still.

More than my classmates, I wanted to see my teachers. I thought about all the ones with whom I wanted to share my achievements. The ones who helped shape me, made me who I was.

Mr. Page, with his refusal to take chemistry seriously. Mr. Provencher, who started American history by explaining his system for note taking, a system I use to this day. Mr. Garabedian, who required our mathematical proofs to be complete and suggested our lives should be the same.

And then there was Mrs. Lane. Poor Mrs. Lane.

Two weeks into Advanced Placement English, I sat down with her for my personal conference. Mrs. Lane was student-sized, but she dressed severely, her hair wound in a tight bun.

"Stephen. This is neither an essay nor four pages." I recognized the stack she tapped with her index finger.

"Yes. Well. I wrote an essay to get into this class. You know I know how to structure one. I know you know how to structure one. Wouldn't producing more of the same just be redundant? In the story I wrote, I addressed all the ideas we were assigned to discuss."

"You handed in close to 100 pages."

"Yes, well, you gave us two weeks."

She nodded. "Once I could see you were capable of writing four pages, weren't you being redundant when you did so another twenty-four times?"

"Yes. Well, the second chunk of four pages and the tenth chunk of four pages don't show any more knowledge of grammar and spelling than the first four pages. But all these pages together show an arc. Actually, three small arcs, with an overreaching one. I'm not sure how to describe what I've done, at least in technical terms. You're the teacher."

"I've heard that."

"Actually, I'm thinking that this will probably be only the first of seven sections. I'm hoping you will help me learn what it is I'm doing right and what it is I'm doing wrong."

"You die at the end of this."

"Yes. Well, it's figurative. I die at the end of the second section, too. And each of the others. That way I can be reborn out of the ashes of my former selves."

"You've written the entire book?"

"No. You only gave us two weeks."

She nodded. "I passed out a reading list for which you're still responsible. I'm also going to give you a second list tomorrow. I think you'll find the books enlightening."

Mrs. Lane handed me my paper. "Good luck."

At the time, I hadn't known exactly what she meant by that, but I now believe she was wishing me luck both with my development as a writer and my development as a person.

Within that non-essay on dystopian elements as examined in *Gulliver's Travels*, I'd created a narrative that included passages of sex, violence, and sophomoric philosophy, which probably did more to set her teeth on edge than the other two combined.

Oh, what I put her through. Hundreds upon hundreds of pages in which I explored and experimented, shouted and shrieked.

But Mrs. Lane stayed with me. She never shut me down, never dampened my enthusiasm, never demanded I conform rather than transform. And by the end of that school year, my non-essay was only the first of seven sections comprising a novel. I then went on to write others, continuing to tap the vein of writing as exploration.

Over the years I have published hundreds of short stories and poems, many of them reflecting—and sometimes refracting—

the lessons I learned from my high school teachers. Whenever that happened, I thought about the teacher in question and wondered how he or she would respond to the piece.

In the week preceding the twenty-fifth reunion, I printed a representative sample of my publications, dividing them into manila folders labeled Page, Provencher, and Garabedian. A fourth folder, labeled Lane, contained copies of all the stories and an essay I'd written for the *Greenwood Encyclopedia of Science Fiction and Fantasy: Themes, Works, and Wonders*.

Would she even remember that student conference?

With all the students who passed in front of them, class after class, year after year, would any of the teachers who had figured so strongly in my development know me from Adam?

If they didn't, I could always leave the folders pinned under my arm. Or present them with halting thanks, mumbling about how each had inspired me.

I remembered a surprising number of classmates at my reunion, none of whom I'd seen during the intervening years. None of the teachers was present, and yet I suddenly realized they were very much present in me, and—one would guess— very present in every former student in that room.

Stephen D. Rogers is a highly published writer of fantasy, horror, literary, mystery, personal essays, romance, and science fiction. Over 500 of Stephen's stories and poems have appeared in more than 100 publications. His Web site, *www.stephendrogers.com*, includes a list of new and upcoming titles, as well as other timely information.

The Maestro Returns

Ramon Carver

When I was in my early sixties, I learned that Dean Daniel Sternberg of Baylor's Music School had funded construction of a storage facility at a Cultural Arts Center (CAC) in Temple, Texas, on the condition that his deceased wife's paintings would be stored there as part of the CAC's permanent collection. Since I had once been his student, I volunteered to catalog her work, consisting mostly of large four-by-eight oils on plywood, primarily still-life studies of flowers. The Arts Center rewarded me by asking me to pick up Dean Sternberg and bring him from Waco to Temple for the official dedication of the new facility.

As an undergraduate, I had idolized him, so for weeks prior to seeing him for the first time in over thirty years, I entertained my wife with stories about his genius. I would straighten my posture and adopt an elegant manner, imitate his voice and proper European accent, and regale her with anecdotes about his vibrant reputation at Baylor—particularly his cool, calm demeanor under fire and his reverberating charm. By the time we saw him exit his front door, looking both dapper and serene, we both recognized the very tall, middle-European impresario, as if he hadn't aged at all. As soon as he bowed slightly and gallantly took her hand, his old school gentlemanly/scholarly qualities wowed my wife.

During the long, leisurely drive from Waco, conversation flowed from one topic to another, and then—just as we were taking the interstate off-ramp to Temple—he asked, offhandedly, "So, Ramon. Did you take any music courses when you were at Baylor?"

I was stunned!

Not only had I studied under him for years, I had dutifully and enthusiastically attended his small orchestral conducting class for two semesters. I had studied Russian in his language classes for a year. Not only had I been in his oratorio chorus and opera classes, I was one of his star performers! I had sung the role of Yamadori in a production of *Madame Butterfly*, and during a matinee performance, when I kneeled down, my flip-flops came off. The audience couldn't see what had happened, and, since Dean Sternberg was busy conducting, neither could he, but surely he had seen the startled look on my face and known that something was amiss—a few memorable looks had been exchanged! Somehow I wiggled back into my flip-flops, and arose without anyone being the wiser, not even the Dean, but surely he remembered that momentary look of sheer panic? That near disaster?

And not only did he not remember that performance, he didn't remember *me* as a former student! Not remember *me?*

I was so taken aback, my jaw dropped open, and I almost drove off the road. "But Dean Sternberg, I was a music *major!*"

The poor gentlemanly man seemingly didn't know how to respond.

We were both silent for a few moments, glanced back and forth at each other wordlessly. Finally, I said, "Well, I was one of thousands, right? I understand perfectly that you can't remember us all. I taught for many years, and I don't remember all my students."

Silence again.

Then he shook his head and almost sang, "But I *do* remember you, Yamadori. I never hear *Butterfly* without thinking of you."

Oh, wow! Faith restored! All he had forgotten "momentarily," he explained, was that I had been one of his music majors.

The dedication of the building commenced without incident, and on the way back to Waco, we reminisced about the performance at Baylor of Walton's *Belshazzar's Feast* during which he lost his place in the music while conducting and fell back on the device he'd taught us in conducting class: "Just keep your hand going around and around and no one will know you've lost your place!"

I also pulled a few mangled words of Russian phrases out of my dusty memory bank so he would know I'd paid attention in his class. And then I told him that singing in the chorus of Bach's *St. Matthew Passion* was one of the highlights of my college years, and he responded by saying, "Turn here, Yamadori, this is the street where I live."

He said goodbye by graciously kissing my wife's hand and thanking me for cataloging his wife's paintings and for transporting him to the event. And then he turned and looked straight into my eyes. "I remember very distinctly the performance when your flip-flops came off, but I didn't learn about it until afterwards because you covered it so well." He laughed, waved goodbye and almost danced toward his house, whistling "One fine day . . ." from *Butterfly*.

I've long since retired from teaching, and I've forgotten the names of 99 percent of my students. But honestly, I remember most of them.

Honest!

It's only their names I've forgotten.

Dr. Ramon Carver is a graduate of Yale Drama School, where he received the MCA Fellowship & Wm. Morris Agency Fellowship. His plays have been produced off-Broadway, *Ain't Nobody Loves You Like a Mama But Your Mama*; in Los Angeles, *A Little Love & Affection*; and elsewhere. As a travel writer, he's published *Best & Worst Travels*, and *What You Need to Know Before You Go*. Retired after thirty years teaching in the United States and abroad, he lives with his wife, Barbara, in Salado, Texas.

The Measure of a Woman

Tanya Ward Goodman

From the moment in 1985 that I walked through the door to her room at Albuquerque's Manzano High School, I knew being in Joyce Briscoe's English class was going to be a unique experience. Not many women in this part of New Mexico wore a T-shirt on which a teary woman exclaimed, "Oops, I forgot to have children!" On a teacher it was surprising, particularly when paired with a prim brown skirt and rather ladylike navy blue, high-heeled pumps.

Her reddish hair was cut short, and she had a habit of tucking it back behind her ears as though even one stray strand might prove a distraction from the task of molding young minds. She explained that she had taken her husband's name, but she drew the line at Mrs. "I am Ms. Briscoe to you," she proclaimed, dragging out Mzzzz, pointing to it as written on the board, and giving us a brief lecture on women's liberation.

She expected our undivided attention. To make her point, she removed the clock from the wall—as she must have done every year—and outlawed wristwatches. "If I see you checking the time," she warned, "I'll think that I haven't given you enough to do." Throughout the year as she sensed our distraction, she would fix us with a hard stare from behind wire-rimmed glasses and urge us not to waste her time or our own.

She passed out outdated flyers, tests from previous classes, and expired theatre posters. "We will not be buying any lined, three-hole paper or notebooks for this class," she said. "It's wasteful and unnecessary. We'll use recycled paper for all tests, essays, and assignments. Without lines on the page, I expect your minds to roam more freely." At the end of the year, she refused to buy a yearbook because she found them "overly sentimental and a waste of paper." Instead, she gave us indelible markers and told us to write our original thoughts, testaments to her cleverness, warm wishes, and—if we must—silly jokes on the walls of her classroom.

Ms. Briscoe had an innate understanding of the myopic nature of high school students, and she made it her mission to lift our eyes from our own navels long enough to gaze at the world around us. She made it clear that she expected us to do our best and nothing less. "You're all smart kids," she stressed. "And it's my job to make sure you learn to use those brains for something good, something productive, something that might actually matter in the world."

Ms. Briscoe took us on many of what she affectionately called "enforced cultural encounters." We attended a local Greek festival, where we tasted spanakopita and joined in boisterous folk dancing. We dined *en masse* at one of Albuquerque's few Chinese restaurants to sample dim sum lunches. On several occasions, we crowded into The Guild, a rag-tag independent theatre long overshadowed by the towering Cineplex, to watch French films. Before and after every outing, Ms. Briscoe provided historical and cultural perspective and urged us to reach beyond our constricted, everyday universe to embrace diversity. She expected us to participate, pay attention, and then be ready to conduct intelligent conversations about each experience. She taught us how to see beyond the surface and how to use discernment when evaluating art and diverse culture. Because she firmly believed it would foster respect for people and lifestyles different from our own, she always stressed the importance of living in the real world and experiencing as much of it as possible

The lessons were refreshingly original, always thought provoking, and often extremely entertaining. When we read *Moby Dick*, she came dressed in blue sailor dress and used it to spark discussion. When we read *Hamlet*, she brought in the soundtrack of *Hair*, played "Oh What a Piece of Work Is Man," and then asked us how it related to Hamlet, the man. When we read *Heart of Darkness*, she brought in *Apocalypse Now* and then delivered a list of topics for discussion that centered on the morality of war. Though she took the work of Melville, Shakespeare, and Conrad with the utmost seriousness—reading and rereading everything along with her students every year—she suffused them with vitality and found ingenious ways to make them relevant to the world we lived in. While other teachers used lesson plans, homework assignments, and tests to foster learning, Ms. Briscoe used costuming, Broadway scores, and Hollywood or foreign films to help us to understand that we constantly draw from the past to create the future. She wanted us to have vision, a sense of moral responsibility, the ability to think independently, and, above all, the ability to speak and write eloquently on subjects that mattered—and she did it all through innovative methods loosely linked to the traditional English curriculum.

Ms. Briscoe loved her students and showed it by treating us like young adults who were capable of reaching far beyond the perimeters of our family, neighborhood, city, and country. She loved us enough to go the distance when it came to providing a stimulating learning experience. She was tough, like an army sergeant with a sense of humor, a flair for drama, and a passionate heart. Although she professed an aversion to hugging, Ms. Briscoe looped an arm around my shoulders when Northwestern University accepted me as a student. "This is a grand opportunity," she said, giving me a quick, tight squeeze and then releasing me. "I expect you to make the best of it."

When we graduated, Ms. Briscoe stood at the end of the receiving line to shake our hands. "You may now call me Joyce," she said, smiling. She handed each of us a card with her phone number on it. "You can call me any time, for any reason, as long as it's not to jibber jabber about silly things. You may *always* call me if you need me." I carried her card in my wallet until I graduated from college; I carried it long after it was so frayed and worn I couldn't see the number any more; I carried it because it reminded me that Joyce Briscoe still had my back. And that meant everything.

Tanya Ward Goodman is a freelance writer and full-time mother. She lives with her family in Los Angeles. She is currently working on a memoir chronicling her experience with her father and his progressive Alzheimer's disease.

Five-Dollar Gloves

Alyssa Baumann

It had escaped my attention completely, as being poor escapes the attention of most third-graders. After all, I had clothes, even if they were third-generation hand-me-downs and out of style. My family had a house, even if it wasn't fancy and meant sharing a bedroom with both of my older sisters. And my mother always had dinner on the table, even if it was a pot of red beans that we doused with ketchup. I had everything I needed, so I failed to notice we were poor. But Mrs. Cole noticed, and it must have broken her heart.

I met her on my first day of third grade at West Elementary School in Weatherford, Oklahoma, in 1985. Mrs. Cole addressed her students on that day the same way she would address us all year: warmly, enthusiastically and with an inviting smile; a smile that looked more like laughter; a smile that lit up her entire face, including her dark brown eyes; a smile that melted her students' hearts.

Shortly after the start of the school year, I celebrated my ninth birthday. I did notice my mother's great effort to have everyone focus on the party and the decorations, rather than notice the torn vinyl on our dining room chairs or the frayed edges of our sagging plaid couch. Since my birthday preceded Halloween by ten days, my mother had draped orange and black streamers from the ceiling, hung smiley-face pumpkin decals on the walls, and baked my favorite cake: chocolate with whipped chocolate frosting and a generous sprinkling of marshmallow cream pumpkins on top. We played pin the tail on the donkey, opened my presents, downed the cake and scoops of vanilla ice cream, and then sprawled on the floor as my mother read a story. Then, one by one, parents arrived to pick up my friends. Soon after everyone cleared the party, the phone rang.

After a brief and rather cryptic conversation, my mother placed the phone back in its cradle. A few minutes later, a car stopped in front of our house, and my mother went out to talk with the driver, who apparently didn't want to come in. Growing curious, I pressed my face against the pane and peered through the front window. Our visitor was Mrs. Cole! Before I could react, I saw my mother accept three large, puffy plastic bags.

Mrs. Cole drove away, and as soon as my mother came in, she carried the bags to our bedroom and plopped them on the floor. Clothes came tumbling out—shirts, pants, shorts, belts, and even shoes! "Mrs. Cole's daughters outgrew all these clothes, and she hated to see them go to waste," my mother nonchalantly announced. My sisters and I rifled through them grabbing the ones we thought would fit us. I pulled out several outfits that fit perfectly, and by the end of the night, my wardrobe had tripled!

Not long after, our class took a field trip to the movie theater. I sat next to my close friend Jill. As the lights dimmed and the screen came alive with images, Jill whispered, "Alyssa, are you poor?" I slouched deeper into my chair, wishing I could disappear and praying that no one heard her. But Mrs. Cole clearly did. She whipped around so quickly and gave Jill such a stern look that Jill clammed up and sank into her chair as I had. But her silence didn't dismiss the pang of her comment. I looked at Jill and uttered a defensive, almost defiant, "No," but I also realized that my teacher knew the truth.

Eventually, autumn's crisp weather gave way to the biting cold of an Oklahoma winter. With it came Christmas, and all the expectations of gift giving and receiving that we both loved and dreaded. By then, Mrs. Cole and I had bonded in a special way, a way I didn't see her bond with other students. I desperately wanted to give her something special.

When I accompanied my mother on a trip to the drugstore, I begged her to let me buy a Christmas present for Mrs. Cole. My mother's face creased with worry, and her posture slouched ever so slightly. She paused, most likely calculating how much money remained in her dwindling bank account, then crossed a few items off her list, items I had not seen her place in her cart. "Okay," she finally agreed, "you can spend five dollars."

I was elated until we wandered up and down the aisles searching for a present, and I realized that the best I could afford was a pair of plain cotton gloves. They didn't seem special enough for Mrs. Cole, and inside I worried that she would know they were all I could afford.

I reluctantly settled on the gloves. Though they didn't exactly live up to my hopes, I wrapped the present in the prettiest paper we had and taped on the shiniest bow I could find in my mother's plastic bag of used bows and ribbon.

The next day I couldn't wait to give the gorgeous package to Mrs. Cole. When I walked up to her desk and held it out, her entire face lit up as though she just received her very first present. "You got me a present?" she beamed. "Thank you! Did you wrap this yourself? Yes, I can tell. You did a beautiful job!" Then, she set my gift aside to take home, as she did with all the presents that day. Part of me was disappointed, but another part of me was relieved that I might not see her bright smile disappear when she opened it. I worried for days afterward that my five-dollar gloves would disappoint her. I also worried about what Jill, and the other kids, had wrapped in their packages.

A few weeks later, drowning in a sea of mittens, wool hats, and oversized coats, the whole school scurried outside to the playground for our first recess back from Christmas break. Wrapped in her heavy wool coat, thick wool scarf, and knee-high boots to shield against the bracing cold, Mrs. Cole stood watch over her third-grade students. I was in the middle of a heated game of tag when I noticed she was trying to catch my attention. I skipped over to where she rocked from one foot to the other to try to keep warm, my own cheeks rosy from the cold. "Whew, it's cold!" she exclaimed through chattering teeth. "I'm glad I brought my gloves out here." I watched as she removed her hands from her pockets and spread her fingers in front of me. She smiled, and I could feel the frozen ground beneath my feet thaw. I was thrilled. Mrs. Cole always dressed in nice dresses and wore equally pretty earrings and shoes. With all the cognizance of a nine-year-old, I realized that she purposefully wore the thin cotton drugstore gloves to the playground—in freezing temperatures—just to let me know my gift mattered.

In many ways, Mrs. Cole was an ordinary schoolteacher in a small, dusty Oklahoma town. She didn't save my life or give hers for mine, or anyone else's. All I have to do, though, is remember her waiting in a car until my friends left my party, or the way she smiled when I gave her those five-dollar drugstore gloves to realize she was extraordinary. And in those days, when a trip to the corner store for penny candy was a luxury in my family, I often wonder who paid for my movie ticket on that fateful field trip.

Well done, Mrs. Cole.

Alyssa Baumann received a bachelor's degree in English from Arizona State University. Currently, she is working on a series of young adult mysteries. She lives with her two best friends—her husband and her dog—in Cave Creek, Arizona.

When the One Great Scorer Comes
(Grantland Rice)

John Forrest

The final horn sounded in my mind. The fans rose as one to cheer our victory, our bench cleared en-mass, and the on-ice celebration began. We were winners; but it was the end. As a team we would never play another game for The Coach. Order was being restored when I spotted his tall figure standing alone at the gate to our players' box. I knew he would not join us on the rink. Retrieving the game puck from the melee, I skated to him and proffered it.

As I began taping the poem to my son's bedroom mirror, the memories came flooding back.

His name was Frank Danby, but to me he will always be "The Coach."

The Coach took on the task of forming a new ice-hockey team with a group of teenagers that was literally a 1950s version of Disney's *Mighty Ducks*.

We were not his first hockey team, but we would be his last. Most of us were local boys. Some were new to the league, and some were castoffs, cut from established teams in neighboring communities. We reflected a wide range of size, talent, and personalities. A few were very good players, and a lot more were boys who wanted to be good but had a long way to go. Yet from scorers to checkers, we were The Coach's team, and he believed in each of us. No one who gave his best was ever cut or benched just to help us win.

Ice-time was scarce in those days, and older age teams drew the worst practice times. Ours was brutal—Saturday mornings at 6:30 A.M. When we whined, The Coach responded by convincing the arena's manager to let us on earlier, and then challenged us to skate with him at 5:30 A.M.! Although he was in his sixties, The Coach always beat us to the ice, and even though some of us arrived a little worse for wear, straight from Friday-night parties, no one ever considered skipping one of those two-hour practices.

I can still feel the frigid arena air clutching my lungs during warm-up circuits. We didn't have to wear helmets in those days, and as we ran our drills, the heat would rise from our heads, forming vaporous halos in the freezing air above. We would skate, shoot, and check to the point of exhaustion and then beg to be allowed to scrimmage for the pure joy of it. And at the end, when the skates came off and warmth began to seep slowly back into our numbed feet, we experienced the delicious agony of tingling toes. Every Saturday, without fail, The Coach was there, teaching and guiding us through our paces. He honed what physical skills we possessed, and he set an example for us in his attitude toward sport and life. For him, winning wasn't everything, nor the only thing—how you played the game was!

I can picture him still. A tall, gaunt, figure stooped slightly at the shoulders, towering above us behind the players' bench; fedora pushed slightly up on his forehead, hands clasped loosely behind him as he rocked slowly back and forth; his expression thoughtful and all knowing. His voice was low and gravelly, and he spoke in measured tones, with the odd "humph" for emphasis. He rarely yelled, and I don't ever remember him belittling a player or disrespecting an opponent or official. The Coach didn't demand respect; he commanded it! He taught us that if you practiced and played his way—hard, clean, and smart—and gave 100 percent every time you laced up your skates, winning would take care of itself. We believed him, followed his lead, and other teams soon found us tough and disciplined challengers.

Two years in a row we made the playoffs, but two years in a row injuries forced me to sit in the stands and watch in frustration as another team—with perhaps more individual talent, but certainly less character—denied us the championship. Some coaches might have dropped and replaced me, or players who were still learning. Some coaches may have considered themselves cursed and called it quits, but not The Coach. He knew it was just a matter of time.

When we lost our first game of the season the following year, other coaches might have lost faith, but The Coach didn't, and he told us so with no uncertainty. He made us believe in ourselves and assured us our time would come—and he was right. We never lost again. Finally, all that hard work fell into place, and for the next two years we went undefeated for over seventy games. We won two league pennants, two county pennants, and a City of Toronto championship. From that point on, nobody beat The Coach's team.

We were too young to fully comprehend the pride he felt, but I understand now. Pride, not for coaching a winning team, but pride in his ability to successfully transform a group of undisciplined rookies into a team of focused, dedicated, hardworking young men who believed in themselves. The Coach taught us more than hockey skills; he taught us skills for life. And as the years passed, he followed our careers and spoke often of our successes. Almost twenty years later, the measure of our respect for him was evident when former team members called, wrote, and traveled from across the country to honor The Coach on his eightieth birthday.

Today I'm a coach, and my son plays hockey. It was a verse from Kipling that I was taping to his mirror. It read:

"When the one great scorer comes, to mark against your name; it matters not who won or lost, but how you played the game."

—*Grantland Rice*

Well, the one great scorer did come to mark against The Coach's name, and I have no doubts how that score sheet read.

I ran my hand over the paper and tape, smoothing it to the glass, savoring those memories of my final game under The Coach's tutelage.

The Coach took the puck from my hand. Eighteen year old, 200-pound defensemen weren't supposed to cry, so no words were exchanged. The Coach studied it for a moment, turning it slowly in his hand. That battle-scarred black disc represented hundreds of lessons taught and well learned, the achievement of a goal and the end of a journey that would forever mark the lives of a dozen young men. My hero nodded, slipped it into the pocket of his coat, turned and walked slowly down the ramp toward the locker room. Not much of a trophy—but it was enough.

John Forrest retired after thirty-four years as an educator. His short stories have appeared in *Reminisce*, *Good Old Days*, and *Capper's*, as well as *Chicken Soup for the Soul* and *A Cup of Comfort for Inspiration*. His works have aired on the Canadian Broadcasting Channel's Radio One; and he won first place in competitions held by the *Toronto Sun*, the *Orillia Packet and Times*, and the *Owen Sound Sun Times*. He also authored *Angels Stars and Trees, Tales of Christmas Magic*.

Home Is Where the Art Is

Nicole Derosier

At age fifteen, my heart would break for no apparent reason. To my surprise, deep changes were unnerving me. I considered myself a change expert, a regular chameleon. I had lived in ten different houses in four different countries and was currently enrolled in my ninth school, a boarding school in New England. Rolling green hills and playing fields sprawled ahead of me, yet I keenly missed my parents, now living in Germany. Frequent moves had filled my childhood with opportunities and adventure—but also with dispiriting feelings of rootlessness and isolation. I kept my letters home light and cheerful and gamely wrestled with my doubts and fears alone.

In this dark forest of confusion, only one activity provided solace: art. My report card was riddled with Cs and Ds, but always had a bright, shiny A-plus next to Art—the one thing I knew I could do, and do well. My notebooks were filled with pages of sketches and doodles, math equations written with calligraphic flair, renderings of historic battles, and portraits of literary characters. Somehow, in a rare moment of clear thinking, I immediately signed up for a new art class, confident it would become a powerful antidote to the unhappiness that consumed me.

The day I walked in to Mrs. Wynne's art studio, a wave of raw emotion washed over me, so intensely I felt weak. A knot of relief tears constricted my throat. I had found sanctuary.

A long wall of leaded glass windows allowed the light of early spring to slant down into the room, infusing it with a warm glow, beaming dusty sunlight onto plastic pails of ceramic glazes, buckets of earth-scented clay, and jars of paintbrushes. Piles of cream-colored muslin lay in an inviting heap, ready to be transformed into brightly colored textiles with the help of the colorful fabric dyes that waited in shallow tubs nearby. Reams of paper and cardstock, rolls of rice paper, stacks of silk-screen frames, and an enormous printing press occupied the far side of the room. Along the back wall, three squat and well-used pottery wheels stood, their bases surrounded by halos of dried clay spatters. The low shelves behind them held clay items left to harden, while the higher shelves stored bisque-fired pieces waiting to be glazed.

I stood stock still breathing in the heady scents that soothed my soul—warm wax, linseed oil, turpentine, paint, damp clay, and the hot, dusty odor of a kiln—and then scanned the walls, where students had hung beautiful batik fabric panels in a dazzling display. The multicolored banners rippled gently under the breeze of an ancient ceiling fan. They were dyed vibrant tones—deep berry pink, emerald green, tropical aquamarine, and stunning cobalt—and undulating white lines of crackled wax, like silken stained glass, delineated their patterns.

"Aren't they absolutely beautiful?"

I was startled out of my worshipful reverie by a soft-spoken voice and turned to see a slender, graceful, silver-haired woman with merry blue eyes.

"They are amazing," I said, patting my heart. "I can hardly wait to make one."

Mrs. Wynne smiled, her bright eyes twinkling. "I am so glad you are here. I can tell you belong in the art studio."

Over the ensuing weeks, I virtually lived in the art studio. As each semester ended, I made sure to sign up for Mrs. Wynne's next class—no matter when it occurred or what it was. I took every class she taught and developed a wealth of skills: hand-building, wheelwork, printmaking, etching, linocut, silkscreen, mono-printing, textile design, batik, block prints, even basic sewing.

In each class, Mrs. Wynne treated each student with equal kindness and respect. She always made time for each of us and was always positive, affirming, and encouraging—never, not even on her worst day, judgmental, sarcastic, or impatient. I felt especially grateful that she kept the studio open all day, into the evenings, and on weekends, so that I could indulge my creative journeys and create work that truly reflected my best efforts.

For weeks I had labored over a detailed clay sculpture of a griffin, carefully fashioning each feather of the wings, each talon of its claws, each scale on its neck. To my horror, the sculpture exploded during firing. When we opened the kiln and discovered the shattered remains, Mrs. Wynne and I hunched together, both shedding tears over the loss. The fact that she cared so deeply about its destruction, and understood my disappointment, inspired me to try harder. Reinvigorated and determined, I spent a week reconstructing the griffin—shard by jagged shard—until it was whole once again. When I proudly showed it to Mrs. Wynne, her delight and praise warmed my weary soul.

But never one for riding on past success, Mrs. Wynne urged me to push beyond what I knew, to try new things without fearing failure, such as learning to make wheel-thrown bowls using delicate white porcelain (instead of traditional red-brown clay) or to create large block-print tapestries that were put on display in the halls of the school. Whenever I created something notable, original, or exceptional, Mrs. Wynne displayed the work in a place of honor—on a shelf in her private office.

When graduation arrived—thanks to art and Mrs. Wynne—despite my mediocre academic record, I was not only graduating but had already been accepted at an art college. I wasn't going to win any awards, but I clapped vigorously for students who claimed Latin awards, physics prizes, varsity letters in athletics, Honor Society certificates, Merit Scholar pins, and all manner of praise and commendation. Instead of feeling lost or left out, I happily daydreamed about the next art studio and all the creations that lay ahead.

Suddenly, the student next to me grabbed my arm, shook me, and virtually shouted, "Go up there! They called your name!"

I stared at him blankly for a moment before looking up at the stage, where Mrs. Wynne stood at the podium, looking straight into my eyes and brightly smiling. I stumbled up the aisle, past my applauding classmates and friends, past my beaming parents, and past the teachers who had wrung their hands with worry over me. When a voice through the loudspeaker announced that I was the recipient of our school's award for excellence in art, I felt wildly excited and equally faint. I reached Mrs. Wynne who handed me the award, hugged me warmly, and whispered, "I am so proud of you. The art room will not be the same without you. You will be missed!"

I finally knew what it meant to be seen, to truly belong.

Nicole Derosier is a graduate of the Corcoran College of Art and Design and currently works out of her studio in her home in Connecticut, where she lives with her husband and three young sons. Over twenty years later, she remains deeply thankful that her teacher, mentor, and friend, Mrs. Gail Wynne came into her life. View Derosier's artwork online at *http://Artshapedworld.4t.com*.

Sister Mary Lucretia

Jim Shannon

Sister Mary Lucretia didn't like me. I could tell by the way she called on me. She looked charitable when she called on my fifth-grade classmates. When she called on me, however, her face puckered, as if my name tasted sour in her mouth. And even if she smiled, it never seemed to soften the piercing blue eyes behind her wire-rimmed glasses.

I didn't know why she didn't like me, or what I may have done to deserve it. But at a time when grownups thought nuns were never wrong, it didn't matter. It couldn't be her fault that she didn't like me; it had to be mine.

This awareness quickly began to take its toll. When she called on me, my brain fogged. Afraid I'd do or say something that would make her like me even less, I found it safer to clam up. Sometimes I remained silent so long she'd give up and call on someone else. And when I did attempt an answer, I developed a stutter, as if I suddenly needed to repeat the beginning of words to give me time to order them correctly in my head.

I'd always been a good student, but Sister Mary Lucretia's apparent disdain filled me with doubt. Maybe I had reached my peak and was morphing into someone else, someone like Jeff or Sally, the kids who never knew the answers to anything. They'd been like that from kindergarten, but maybe for some people mental roadblocks hit later, like in fifth grade.

To add to my misery along came October and with it a poem, "October's Bright Blue Weather," written by Helen Hunt Jackson in the late eighteenth century. The poem was eight four-line stanzas long and was too full of bumblebees and Gentians, whatever they were, and comrades who "seek sweet country haunts," which sounded suspiciously like Communists to me. What was worse, Sister Mary Lucretia insisted we memorize it. Our memorization was broken into a stanza a day, with the whole class standing to recite as much as we'd learned. The first and second days' stanzas went easily. On the third day, we had all tolled off the first three stanzas and sat back down when Sister Lucretia paused and said, "Jeff, stand please. And Sally. And . . ." From behind the wire-rims, those searching blue eyes roamed the room, and I looked down, knowing where they were going to stop, even before I heard her say, "Jimmy, stand. Would you all please recite the three stanzas again?"

Feeling wobbly from the rush of heat flushing my cheeks, I pulled myself to a standing position and placed my hands gingerly against my thighs. Everyone knew Sally and Jeff wouldn't know the three stanzas. By choosing me, Sister Lucretia had lumped me in with them, letting my classmates know—in case they hadn't yet noticed—that I wouldn't come through either. The irony was I'd memorized the whole poem, all eight stanzas, as a desperate hedge against my suddenly untrustworthy memory and obviously shrinking brain.

Embarrassed and with my eyes focused on the floor, I might not have ever gotten off the ground had Sally and Jeff not launched into the first stanza. Three days of everyone repeating it had apparently fixed the beginning in the two's minds. I joined on line three, and we marched into the second stanza. Two lines in, they lapsed into silence and, momentum on my side, I managed to finish alone. I also finished the third stanza quickly and alone, and then I distinctly heard Sister Mary Lucretia say, "Thank you, Jimmy."

When I looked up from the floor and into her eyes, I'm not sure what I saw there, or what shifted in me, but I suddenly felt tired of the whole situation, tired of her not liking me, tired of being afraid of her. Fully aware I was plunging into uncharted and dangerous waters, I took a deep breath, focused on the top of the wall just above her head, and leaped into stanza four. A few students near me looked up, probably wondering if I'd misunderstood how much of the poem we were supposed to memorize. By stanza five, my classmates' growing anxiety was palpable. Reciting stanza four might have been a simple mistake, but charging into stanza five definitely signaled defiance—to a nun, no less! My classmates now squirmed in their seats. Those closest to me leaned away, as if trying to put some distance between themselves and the kid who was obviously bent on committing fifth-grade suicide.

My voice may have momentarily wavered, but my determination did not. I squared my shoulders and barreled through stanza six. And seven came easily because I remembered the parts about the Communists looking for a place to haunt. I finished eight, the concluding stanza, in double-time, the words rattled off by rote with no emphasis or sense of understanding. But what mattered to me was that they were the right words, as clear to me as if they were written on the top of the wall where my eyes were fixed.

Then, enduring absolute silence, I slowly looked down at Sister Mary Lucretia and was astonished to see that she was smiling. And not just with her lips. Those fiery blue eyes seemed to be dancing behind her wire-rims. I had defied her, yet she looked as if I'd just given her the best present ever.

"Thank you, Jimmy. Very good. Very, *very* good."

I was more confused than ever. I thought I'd condemned myself but found instead I had somehow managed to free myself. Now, she liked me. No doubt about it. Maybe she always had but, if not, my recitation had clearly changed her mind.

From that moment I stopped fogging up, stopped stuttering, and became the student I'd always been. I also became a schoolyard hero for a little while—the kid who'd taken on a formidable teacher and gotten away with it. Even though I enjoyed the notoriety, I was smart enough not to try that stunt again.

But it was almost twenty years before I finally understood what had *actually* happened. And it all came together in another classroom, where, now, I was the English teacher with the big desk in front of the room. Up to that point, I was still standing up there like I was reciting poems I'd memorized, trying to show my students how smart I was. Then one day, during a quarterly writing celebration, when everyone in my sophomore class shared something he or she had written, I read them my tale of fifth-grade defiance. They seemed to like it, but one comment took me aback. It came from a quiet girl, who said, "That was really understanding of her, to know you needed to do that."

"What do you mean?" I was really puzzled.

"Well, she could have stopped you at any time, couldn't she?"

"I guess so." Sister Mary Lucretia could have shut me up by just clearing her throat.

"But she let you defy her," the girl said. "If the other kids in the class knew that's what you were doing, she must have known it too."

She was right. All along, I'd thought the story, which I'd recounted way too many times, was about my defiance. But it was really about more than that. It was about a wise teacher who understood that I needed to prove I had a brain and was willing to allow me to openly challenge her authority to bolster my confidence.

And now, here was one of my students explaining to me the part of the lesson I'd somehow missed. This time around, I learned it. I stopped needing to be the smartest person in my classroom and began focusing on what my students needed to be. And I owed it all to Sister Mary Lucretia, whose wisdom allowed me to be the smartest person in the classroom on the one day I really needed to be.

Jim Shannon is a retired high school teacher who now teaches part-time at a community college. His writing has been published in magazines as varied as *Mad* and *TV Guide*, and he has had stories appear in *Alfred Hitchcock Mystery Magazine*, as well as in the anthologies *Seasmoke* and *Still Waters*.

Against All Odds

Elaine Ingalls Hogg

When I was five or six years old, I remember hoisting myself up on the tipsy circular stool that sat in our front room. Once up, my legs wouldn't reach the floor, so I crawled down, and with one foot, tried to pump the worn pedal in order to elicit a beautiful sound from my mother's beloved organ.

Later, when I was tall enough to reach the pedals, I wanted to take professional organ lessons, but I suffered a serious illness, and the resulting medical bills left my parents with no money to pay for private lessons. However, by that time, I had fallen in love with music, and the desire to learn how to play an instrument burned brightly.

Twenty years later, I was a newcomer to Port Hawkesbury, a small town in Nova Scotia, Canada.

My children were finally in school, which meant that I finally had enough free time to pursue my long-lost childhood dream. I still fervently wanted to learn music and how to play an instrument, but now I wanted to play the piano, and this time no one, or nothing, would deter me.

The day of my first lesson, I waited nervously on the front step for someone to answer my knock. "Come in," a faint voice called from the other side of the door. Timidly, I turned the brass doorknob and crept into the foyer, but I couldn't see anyone. *You must be imagining things,* a voice inside me seemed to say. I worried that I might have the wrong house and was trespassing. I turned to leave, but before I could close the door behind me, I heard someone say one more time, "Come in, please. I'm in the kitchen."

"I'm sorry to disturb you, I must have come to the wrong house," I said, apologizing for the intrusion. I couldn't help noticing her slender misshapen, crooked fingers or her wheelchair. I couldn't imagine any way she could possibly play the piano. She smiled but said nothing. "I'm Elaine, and I was looking for Helen MacDonald, the piano teacher," I explained hurriedly.

"I'm Helen MacDonald," she answered, her smile now wide and welcoming. "If you will kindly push my chair up to the piano in the living room, we'll begin your lesson now."

Over the course of time, Helen shared with me that she, too, had fallen in love with music as a child. She particularly loved the jigs and the reels of her Scottish heritage, but when she heard classical music streaming out of the small brown radio on a shelf in the living room, she told her mother she, too, wanted to take piano lessons. Unfortunately, she always received the same reply. "Helen I know that's what you'd like to do, but right now I don't have the money to pay for your lessons."

Like my mother, Helen's mother, Mrs. Arsenault, didn't say this to discourage her daughter. Since her husband's untimely death, she was also having a hard time providing for her family's needs. The years passed, and by the time Helen became a teenager, for the most part, she forgot about her dream. "I had waited so long I was convinced that even if I did have the opportunity to take lessons, it was too late to gain the finger dexterity needed to play classical music," she explained, with only a hint of wistfulness.

When she was fifteen years old, however, she finally had an opportunity to take lessons. "I don't wish to brag, but I was a natural," she said, sighing. "My long, flexible fingers flew over the keys as though I had been taking lessons for a lifetime." In three short years she finished the requirements needed in order to take the Royal Conservatory Teacher's Exam, which she passed a short time later. For the next few years, her dreams had truly come true—she was living her passion for music. She spent hour after hour perfecting her craft, but when she was in her early twenties, she faced a tragic setback.

She began experiencing stiffness in her joints, which was ultimately diagnosed as rheumatoid arthritis, a disease that soon robbed her of her former dexterity. It progressed rapidly and soon cruelly ravaged her body, completely crippling her hands and feet. The day I met her, although she was still quite young, with many years ahead to develop her craft, she could no longer walk or play the piano.

Despite her misfortune, she refused to surrender her love for music. She used her understanding of the art and her ability to listen and give instruction to coach students. Week after week, for years, she offered me her wisdom, her talent, and her enthusiasm. With her encouragement, I was able to pass my advanced piano exams, become a music teacher, and share the gift of music with others for the next thirty years.

And oddly enough, that first day was the only day I ever remember thinking of Helen as disabled. Very quickly I realized that her abilities and her passion for music surpassed the physical limitations she had to suffer. Together, we fulfilled our childhood dreams and forever shared a mutual love for music that fed our souls and allowed our spirits to soar in unison above the Nova Scotia sky.

Elaine Ingalls Hogg taught piano for thirty years. Later in life she also became a writer and has been published in more than a dozen anthologies, and several magazines. Two of her books were best sellers and another, *Remembering Honey,* won an award from the Canadian Authors' Association in 2000.

Mrs. Ray and the Class Clown Conquer the Classics

V. S. Anderson

English class came after lunch, when full stomachs made us sleepy. Mrs. Ray was a tiny, doll-like woman with dyed red hair. "English," she said in her operatic voice, "entails far more than simply reading books, plays, or poetry, and far more than merely writing correctly. English is the art of communication, a supreme act of reason."

We blinked, yawned, looked around at each other, and focused more on Bobby, our perpetual class clown, who was, as usual, trying to poke a pencil through a hole in the floor.

"English is an art form, both in the written word and in the spoken language," Mrs. Ray concluded and then looked out at us as if she knew all of our deepest secrets.

Bobby's activities had not gone unnoticed. She calmly walked back to where he was continuing to twist a pencil into a hole in the wooden floor, unaware that he had been found out. "Drilling for oil?" Mrs. Ray inquired, looking down at his bent form.

Bobby remained so preoccupied with his efforts to break through to the room below that he didn't seem to hear Mrs. Ray, or at least he didn't respond. In the best of times, we all seemed to breathe as one, so when Mrs. Ray stood over Bobby, we collectively held our breath and silently stared at the petite woman and the tall muscular giant of a boy at the back of the room.

"Robert," she repeated. "Are you drilling for oil?"

Bobby sat up, but was so tall, even when sitting, he was eye to eye with Mrs. Ray. "Err, no ma'am, I . . . well, no ma'am." He abandoned the pencil and offered no excuse or explanation. He just sat there waiting for the all-too-frequent reprimand and detention sentence that typically followed.

"Robert," she said, gently, yet firmly.

"Everyone calls me Bobby," he replied sheepishly.

"In my class you shall always be Robert. Now, Robert, for tomorrow, I would like for you to write an essay on what it is that you hoped to accomplish by excavating a hole in this floor."

We let out our breath and giggled. No one liked to see Bobby in trouble—again. He was almost six feet tall and big—not fat, muscular. Even though he towered over us and his size intimidated us, he was like a walking tree, a gentle, sandy-haired boy with dark brown eyes. Behind his back, too many kids made fun of him and some even rudely called him "dummy" to his face before scampering away.

Mrs. Ray turned to face the rest of the class and smiled, not a tight-lipped smile, a wide, toothy smile that became her trademark. Looking back at Bobby for a moment, and then skimming her eyes around the room and connecting with eyes looking back at her, she said, "I want each of you to write an essay on why you thought having Robert write an essay was so humorous. Robert, I will accept a 200-word essay from you, and as for the rest of you, I require a 500-word essay—not a word less."

As she headed back to the front of the room, we collectively groaned and grumbled to one another in low tones about how unfair she was being. As if she had internal radar that could hear a gnat and zoom in on it within milliseconds, she snapped around and glared at us. "This," she declared, "is *not* unfair. Robert's actions only affected Robert. On the other hand, your reaction was . . . well, I have high hopes some of you will figure it out and write a brilliant essay about it."

At the end of class, just before she dismissed us, Mrs. Ray calmly said, "Robert, would you please come back to my room after school." It wasn't really a question. Bobby nodded and walked out of the room with his head down.

Once school was over, Bobby approached me and asked me to go back to Mrs. Ray's classroom with him. His request surprised me, but I felt for Bobby, so I went along. Mrs. Ray was seated behind her maple-colored desk. It was wooden and had been moved too many times, which left deep scratches along the side and splinters on the legs. I knew because I stared at it, waiting. Our new English teacher was busily shuffling papers while simultaneously looking at an open book.

"Good, you're here, and you've brought an ally." Mrs. Ray looked into my eyes, as if searching for a name to go with my round face. "And you are?"

"I'm Vickie. I'm in the same class as Bobby."

"Oh, yes, Victoria. Your desk is one of those near the window. How did football practice go today?" She peered over the frame of her reading glasses.

Everyone who sat by the window passed time watching the football team go through its daily exercises, and still I was startled. "Ah . . . I . . ." She arched her eyebrows. "They looked pretty good." I finally said, grateful that she quickly moved on.

"Robert, are you and Victoria good friends? Do you trust each other?"

Bobby looked at me, back at Mrs. Ray, back at me again, and then smiled. "Yes ma'am. Vickie and me, well, we sort of look after each other 'cause, well, 'cause."

Mrs. Ray looked into both of our eyes for what seemed like a very long time, and then nodded. "Please take a seat," she said, pointing to two desks in the front row. "I won't keep you long." Before we could make our first step, she opened the top desk draw and extracted a comic book. "Robert, you don't care much for reading, do you?"

"No, ma'am." He warily dropped his head and shook it back and forth.

"Well, maybe you would like to read this." She held out a comic book version of *The Three Musketeers,* which Bobby happily accepted and thumbed through quickly.

"Let's read some of it aloud," Mrs. Ray suggested, her voice soft and barely more than a whisper. "Then you may take the book home, if you would like to finish it on your own."

As soon as he began stumbling over words, I realized Bobby could barely read. Mrs. Ray's eyes met mine, held my gaze for several long seconds, and then returned to Bobby. Throughout the next fifteen minutes, her face softened, radiating kindness and patience.

After that, Bobby and I often returned to her classroom after school. Under her patient, gentle tutelage, Bobby soon graduated from comic books to real books. As his reading progressed, his clowning diminished. I, too, benefited greatly from those after-school sessions. I learned a lot more than English from Mrs. Ray—she awakened a passion for learning that would last a lifetime.

V. S. Anderson will always view Mrs. Ray as a heroine and credits her for an ongoing passion for writing. She is currently mastering the art of writing short stories and marketing her first novel. She lives in a small town in East Texas with Bogart and Patch, whom she calls her "literary cats" because they love to stretch out across the keyboard as she writes.

Twiggy and the Teacher

T. C. Vratil

Up until 1968, I attended a tiny country school in Kansas and hadn't ventured far beyond the borders of my insular world. Like me, all the teachers at my old school looked as if they were still living in the 1950s. Male teachers greased their hair back and dressed in white shirts and black slacks; female teachers wore beehive hairdos and cotton dresses with matching belts cinched tightly to accentuate their waists, with high-heeled shoes and stockings, replete with the requisite girdles and garters.

For sixth grade, we bussed to a larger school, where I encountered Ms. Jenny Sommers. She wore a flowered, bell-bottomed pantsuit and held her straight, long hair back with a wide headband. Silver hoop earrings dangled from her pierced ears, and dozens of metal bracelets covered both arms. Instead of sitting behind her desk, looking prim and serious, she perched on its front edge, smiling and swinging her feet back and forth.

"Hello! *Hola*! *Bonjour*! *Guten Tag*!" she repeated, cheerfully greeting each student. When the bell rang, she held up a copy of the district's prescribed curriculum. "We won't be needing this," she said, and then tore it into tiny pieces and tossed them into the air where they fluttered around her like confetti. Students audibly gasped, and several boys shouted with joy. She held up a hand that had every finger covered in rings. "Just because we won't be studying from the standard curriculum doesn't mean we won't be working hard!" The boys groaned.

Ms. Sommers taught us about "sit-ins" by having us sit on the floor to discuss controversial topics—like whether or not the Vietnam War was moral or immoral and the social and political ramifications of the assassination of Martin Luther King, Jr., and Senator Robert Kennedy. When they launched Apollo 7, she brought a small television to school so we could discuss space exploration and whether or not it advanced American culture.

Day after day, Ms. Sommers dazzled us and broadened our horizons. Nevertheless, I still preferred lying low and hiding in the background, silently observing. Or at least I thought I was invisible until Ms. Sommers asked me to stay after class.

I was somewhat startled to be singled out and stood in front of her pushing the toe of my shoe against the edge of her desk. She cleared her throat and then stood up and came around the desk. "Teresa, what do you know about Susan?"

"Know about her?" I asked, surprised.

Ms. Sommers smiled. "Well, for instance, do you know if she has any friends?"

"Not that I know of." I could see where this was heading; she was about to ask me to do something that would plummet me to the bottom of the popularity totem pole. Hoping to escape, I inched toward the door. "Uh, I better leave if I'm going to catch my bus."

"Teresa," Ms. Sommers said brightly. "I want us to do something to help Susan."

"Us—as in you and me? Help Stinky Susan?"

Ms. Sommers's eyes flashed a withering look. "I am going to confide in you, and I need you to promise that you won't share this information with anyone else in the class."

My invisibility was diminishing by the second, but who could resist her? I nodded but glanced toward the door as if I could still escape if I hurried.

"Her family doesn't have any running water at home, so they can't bathe as often as we do. And she has only two dresses that she has to rotate. You don't really think she enjoys not being able to smell all fresh and lovely like the rest of you girls, do you?" I bit my lip and met her eyes briefly. "I made arrangements for Susan to come in early to shower in the locker room before school. I know you have an older sister, and I wondered if your mother had extra clothes we might be able to give Susan."

Relief flooded through me so quickly I didn't think before I blurted. "That's it? I don't have to be friends with her?"

Ms. Sommers frowned. "No, Teresa, you don't have to be her friend, but I would like you to do me this one favor."

I ran out the door without answering, but not before I saw the look of disappointment in her eyes. That night my mother and I packed clothes into a grocery sack, which I carried to school and immediately slid under Ms. Sommers's desk before she, or anyone else, saw me. When Ms. Sommers noticed the sack, she didn't say a word; she just looked at me and winked.

The very next day Susan came to school transformed. Not only was she well groomed and wearing my older sister's white blouse and blue flowered skirt, she sat up straighter, her eyes sparkled, and she was smiling, really smiling.

Time spent outside the classroom, however, became a nightmare. Other girls—far more popular girls—had begun to tease me. My "little girl" pedal pushers, my spotless white Keds, and my pigtails sent them into hysterics. They wore mini-skirts, pantyhose, and tight blouses and styled their hair in that perfect little Marlo Thomas flip. The worst came when they discovered that I had not graduated to a bra: They encouraged boys to rush by me and reach up to snap invisible straps.

I stood waiting outside the bathroom door, literally jiggling to forestall a disaster when Ms. Sommers came by and stopped short. "What are you doing, Teresa?"

"Waiting," I mumbled.

"Why? I don't think there's a line." When three of my tormentors came out and scurried down the hallway, I confessed that I had been avoiding the other girls for months. "They're growing up, looking more like you every day . . . but I'm . . . not."

"And they make fun of you?"

I choked back a sob and nodded.

The next day, as everyone was running outside for lunch recess, Ms. Sommers pulled me aside. "Have you ever seen a picture of Twiggy?" I hadn't, so she pulled out a magazine and opened it to a page where a stick thin girl modeled a very hip outfit. "Why don't you take this home?" she suggested, and I left that day gripping *Vogue* magazine against my flat chest.

I begged my mother for weeks to let me cut my hair short, and one day she relented. I went straight from the beauty parlor to the drug store where I bought black mascara with my allowance and pirated it home. The following Monday, after she left for school, I sneakily borrowed one of my sister's dresses, pulled on a pair of her panty hose, and stuffed toilet paper into the toes of a pair of her shoes. For one minute, I considered stuffing one of her bras, but Twiggy didn't need a bra to look very cool.

I don't remember how my classmates responded, but I will never forget the glee I saw in Ms. Sommers's eyes. She squealed with delight. "Stand right there," she said, and then pulled out her Polaroid camera and snapped several pictures. "Oh, that's perfect," she said, winking. "You're looking very Twiggy." She then wrote "My Favorite Twiggy" in her flowing scroll, and handed them to me. "You know, Teresa," she whispered conspiratorially, "Everyone is beautiful in her own special way."

T. C. Vratil was born and raised on a farm in Kansas. She moved an hour away from the family farm and visits often. Her work has been published in the *Kansas City Star*, *Letters to My Mother*, and other anthologies.

The Glorious Madame Fung

Katherine L. Clark

I still remember the day we passed each other along the pink granite walkway of the campus mall. Madame Fung paused to introduce herself and held out her hand, allowing her delicate fingers to rest in mine like a soft sycamore leaf crooking its tiny ribs. Still attractive in her sixties, she exuded Old-World charm and steely grace—an example of that vanishing breed of genteel Chinese who had learned French and English from Catholic nuns in Beijing before knowledge of a Western tongue was considered treason.

I could not tell whether she liked me or not, and yet I found her charming and intriguing. After smiling in a way that didn't offer any clues, she politely asked how I liked teaching in Chengdu.

"The students are very bright," I answered sincerely.

She nodded her head. "How many students are there now in the Department of International Business?" Her voice was smooth as silk.

"One hundred sixteen," I answered, although I was fairly certain she already knew the answer. Like Southern belles, refined Oriental women often cultivate the impression of naiveté when quite the opposite is true. Colleagues had informed me that Madame Fung was happy to advise postgraduates in the accounting department, but she had no interest in teaching Mandarin to foreigners. Even so, something about her gentility emboldened me enough to breach decorum and ask if she would consider tutoring me in Mandarin. "It would honor me," I added, bowing.

If Madame Fung was insulted by my unorthodox request, she showed no signs of it. But fearing rejection unless I impressed her, I forged ahead. "I don't want to speak with a Sichuan dialect. It's so common. I want to learn Mandarin with a dignified Beijing accent, as you speak, Madame Fung."

She laughed and again took my hand. "I also find Sichuan slang an affront to my ears. My family lived in Shanghai, so I have a sense how it feels to be an outsider when you are living in Chengdu."

We agreed to meet on Sundays at her home, where my knocks were always greeted with giggles. "*Qing jin; Qing jin*! Come in! Come In! Please excuse the mess."

She said this, but her house was always immaculate and smelled as fresh as rain. Her favorite flowers, sword lilies, frequently stood in a vase on the bookcase, and the tile floor was polished to a shine. Mementos of her academic career—photographs of her with students in Paris, Melbourne, and North Carolina—were scattered about the room. Graduation portraits of her four daughters, each holding a master's degree or a doctoral diploma, were hung along a wall like a row of medals. Dozens of rewrapped gifts bestowed by universities and foreign businesses rested in a china cupboard next to the piano.

Each week Madame Fung added new vocabulary words and drilled me until my brain ached. A teacher teaching a teacher is like a doctor caring for a doctor—both need the right balance of expertise and cooperation to allow the other to act their role. I demurred to her authority when it came to learning Mandarin and always showed her the greatest respect. Instead of asking her to slow down, I would inquire about the derivation of a word or phrase and that would lead her to pause and think of illustrations that evolved into stories, all of which dropped from her lips like pearls.

On one occasion, Madame Fung told me that her father had been a renowned professor of Chinese literature in Shanghai and that she had often read books about the West in his library. She had enjoyed opportunities to meet foreign teachers, and although teaching would become her profession, Madame Fung, a prodigy on the piano, had dreamed of joining the opera. But her father insisted that his only daughter study practical mathematics and sent her to a boarding school in Beijing, where she fell in love with the son of a family friend.

Unfortunately for Madame Fung, the 1950s brought a period known in Chinese history as the "Hundred Flowers."

A time when Chairman Mao first called Chinese artists and scientists China's "flowers," encouraging the "flowers to bloom," and then abruptly changed his mind and began spying on the same artists and scientists, searching for signs of collaboration with Chiang Kai-shek's Kuomintang army. He arrested over 30,000 intellectuals and condemned them to labor camps. During this time, Madame Fung's fiancé escaped to Formosa with his family.

"We wrote to one another for decades," she told me, tears welling in her eyes. "But when the revolution was over, his family decided not to return, and he never came back to China."

The 1960s were even worse. When we discussed the phrase *shangshan xiaxiang*, she explained that it meant "going to the countryside," not in the sense of having a picnic, but in the context of being exiled by the Communists during the Cultural Revolution. While she and her husband were forced to quit professional jobs to labor in factories and mills, their older girls were *shangshan xiaxiang*—dispatched to work on farms and grow vegetables in the country.

The agricultural communes on the Mainland began to fail, and people in the cities were starving and living in dire conditions. "We had to stitch scraps of cloth and cardboard and glue them together to create shoes," she explained. She then told me that Chairman Mao wanted to cleanse the nation of old thinking, old culture, old customs, and old habits. "So he ordered the Red Guards to invade the homes of educated persons with what he now considered 'bad class' backgrounds. Suddenly teachers were suspect. Confucian ideals were turned upside down, and my family fell from the highest rungs of society to the lowest."

To save their lives, Madame Fung destroyed all evidence of her family's upper-class heritage. Her painted scrolls, antique furniture, and all of their leather-bound books had to be burned. She refused, however, to destroy her beloved piano, a rebellious act that risked banishment.

In 1976, Chairman Mao died, and three years later, Madame Fung was assigned to teach accounting at the Southwest University of Finance and Economics in Chengdu. Even if it was not exactly *shangshan xiaxiang*—as she was not forced to toil in the fields—she was sent to live in the backwaters of Chengdu.

"When I arrived eighteen years ago," she said, "the president of the university was very kind. He needed me at the time, and, therefore, treated me better than most of the teachers. All the same, I did not like the harsh sound of the Sichuan dialect or the boniness of the river fish." She wrinkled her nose in such a way it was clear that life in Chengdu was frequently unpleasant.

She renewed her vitality by working with the students and indulging her love of music. "My husband and I both enjoy singing. Now that he is retired, and we are living together for the first time in many years, we attend a Christian church service every Sunday so that we can sing." When I asked if she had a favorite song, she answered quickly, "Amazing Grace."

Madame Fung refused to accept any compensation for my Mandarin lessons, so before I returned to America, I searched for a gift that would prove useful and not sit rewrapped in the china cupboard with all the others. Because she still considered it impolite to open a present in front of the person who gave it to her, I did not find out until long after I left China that she and her husband often fell asleep listening to the CD I had given her of a Southern Baptist choir singing "Amazing Grace."

Madame Fung will always be a grand lady, albeit one whose glory days, like her beauty, is fading. She exemplifies the finest characteristics of Chinese culture: courage, the willingness to make personal sacrifice, and modesty. She not only endured the Cultural Revolution, she helped her four daughters survive and thrive. As an elegant elderly woman, whose elite ethics have long ago fallen from favor, she is a treasure among those who lived before the days of Chairman Mao. I felt blessed to know her and learned far more than Mandarin under her tutelage.

Katherine L. Clark was recruited from Marietta College in 1997 to teach English at a university in Chengdu, while her family remained in Ohio. She and her husband have since moved to Oregon, where she volunteers as a docent at the Portland Art Museum.

A similar version of Katherine L. Clark's story was originally published in *A Women's Asia* (Travelers' Tales/Solas House, Palo Alto, CA).

Fixer Upper

Victoria R. LaFave

On first meeting, he introduced himself as Fixgrr. He even wrote it that way on the chalkboard, and then turned, grinned, dipped slightly to the side, and flexed his muscles. A Vietnam veteran and former Mr. Michigan competitor, he had a Hulk Hogan physique, complete with the over-sized horseshoe-shaped mustache. His real name was Mr. Fix, and he was a relatively easygoing high school English teacher. But he made an indelible impression, and from then on his students loved to call him Fixgrr, drawing out the "grr" sound, which always made him laugh, particularly since he'd clarified from day one that "the g was silent."

Mr. Fix opened our semester by discussing the art of journaling and set the clock for a ten-minute writing session. "Write about whatever you want," he said, and then paused to admire our befuddled expressions. "Okay, okay, I'll loan you copies of *Far Side* cartoons and famous quotes to spur your imaginations." He'd pass out slips of paper and Xeroxed cartoons and then sit back to watch us labor over our journal entries.

I still have my journals, each filled with my musings and strips of paper bearing Fixgrr's favorite quotes and quirky cartoons. Yellowing Scotch tape holds some of his most powerful words in place. But I don't have to thumb through my journals to remember what he said. Twenty years later, his words hold the same power. "Strip a writer to the buff, point to his scars, and he'll tell you the story of each small one," Fixgrr said often. "From the big ones you get novels. And remember, students, a little talent is a nice thing to have if you want to be a writer, but the only real requirement is the ability to remember the emotional story behind each scar."

His passionate belief that we all had something valuable to say often inspired me to continue writing, particularly when I struggled to find the right words. "Write about what you know!" he would say, chalk dust flying, as he simultaneously scribbled the words on the chalkboard.

Often, while we were writing our morning journal-writing exercise, he walked up and down the aisles between our desks, peering over our shoulders. "Show, don't tell! Miss Kelley," he would tease a girl known for being a bit snoopy. "Now, tell me, is the biker wearing a bandana wrapped around his bald head? Is he just *cold*? Or, does he have *ice crystals* forming on his mustache?"

Moving to the next desk, he'd snap up someone's paper and then swirl around to look at all of us in turn. "What do I always say, class? Right, say it with me." He'd lift his foot and wait for us to join in before crashing it to ground. "Stomp out passive verbs!" Then, he'd run to the chalkboard, his gray hair flying, grab his chalk, and write an example on the board of a passive verb being replaced with an active one. "Look, the sentence is alive!"

I loved almost everything about Mr. Fix's English class; I lived for the literary discussions and his wacky writing suggestions. But I dreaded when he would invite one of us to get up and read one of our journal entries to the class. Of course, no one wanted to volunteer. Like my fellow classmates, I would scrunch down in my chair, avoiding eye contact, until his steely blue eyes would scan the room and invariably pick me. Luckily, he was always particularly sensitive to our obvious feelings of excessive teenage vulnerability, and he always concluded with positive words like "Great use of action verbs," or "Vivid description," or "Way to tap into that emotion." And he always thanked us for sharing a piece of our marvelous lives with the class. He made it cool to be a writer, even for the jocks.

Another amazing thing—he would turn the tables around and tell us that *we* motivated *him*. One spring day, after staring out the window for a long time, mesmerized by the sight of snow melting off the roof, I wrote in my journal about how much I couldn't wait to experience the sights, sounds, and smells of spring—like the smell of campfires burning, the soothing sound of whippoorwills singing, and the beauty of fireflies dotting the night sky.

The following Monday, he handed my journal back to me with these words: "It was a pleasure reading your journal this sunny Sunday morning. Thanks for sharing it with me. This is the last one I'm going to read today because your entry coaxed me into going for a walk in the sun to watch spring being born."

The day after I was cut from the varsity team, I used my journal to vent a morass of angry, hurt, frustrated, and bitter feelings. The next day, Fixgrr returned my journal with an entire paragraph about times he had also suffered disappointment. And he closed with a particularly potent comment designed to lift my spirits. "You're a success waiting to happen, Vicki. Don't forget that!"

And I didn't. I used that exact phrase when my four-year-old daughter labored for hours to build a tall Lego castle, and the whole thing collapsed the minute she opened its tiny door. And when my seven-year-old son struck out in his playground baseball game, those same magical words calmed him.

Last fall, on what was otherwise a typical Monday morning, I received horrible news. The local radio station somberly announced that local teacher Doug Fix had died of a massive heart attack while running in an area race. In 2006, he had finished the Boston Marathon and appeared to be in phenomenal shape, so it came as a shock to everyone. I immediately felt devastated and bereft. I worried that I had never found a way to truly thank him for all the little—and big—things he did to help me grow as a writer, and a human being. Did he know how much his words had inspired me and encouraged me, long after high school was far behind me? Could he possibly have known that every time I received a rejection letter, I remembered his tireless enthusiasm—and more importantly, his faith in me?

I pulled out the last journal I wrote while in his class and flipped to the last page. Luckily, I had written about my feelings of sadness about losing him as a teacher and concluded by saying, "I wish some things never had to end." Fixgrr had drawn a cartoon figure of himself, complete with an exaggerated horseshoe mustache and long hair. The figure had one arm up, with bicep bulging, waving, and he scribbled in the margin "a tiny little wave." That made me laugh! But his final words made me cry. At the bottom of that page, I had written, "The End." In typical Fixgrr fashion, he had boldly crossed those words out and replaced them with, "The Start."

Victoria R. LaFave surrendered her marketing career to pursue writing. With the help of her husband, who takes their two small children to the park so Victoria can have writing time, she has been published in *Parents* magazine and written a children's book, *Lonely Lucas*, inspired by her seven-year-old son Luke.

Observations and Lessons for the Extraordinary Woman

Emma Gordon

We often find teachers in the most unexpected places, at the oddest times, and usually when we don't even know we're looking for them. As a driven young actress who had traveled around the world solo and chose to live in New York City to train and work, I thought I was the last person in need of guidance. I called myself "The little Aussie that could." Even in the wake of being diagnosed with melanoma while thousands of miles away from my family, I was confident I could cope perfectly well on my own. Inevitably, however, my façade began to crumble, and I reluctantly sought help in the form of a Wednesday-night cancer support group at Gilda's Club in Greenwich Village.

Enter Margie Myers. I remember our first meeting clearly. This fabulous woman with fabulous hair and a fabulous outfit moved seats to sit next to me—to console me—and as she held my hand, she said defiantly, "This . . . is my age! I'm twenty-eight. . . . I'm not fifty-eight. . . . I don't know when that happened! Really, when did that happen?" I liked her immediately.

You see, although Margie's body had aged and ovarian cancer had begun to take hold, her spirit had not seen a day over age thirty. She lived out loud. Often I would sneak in late to our group meetings, and I could hear her from halfway down the hall, telling what I was sure was an outrageous story of her days as one of the first wholesale shoe saleswomen on the road. I would open the door to find her acting out the story and the other women practically in tears laughing. When the tears were not from laughter but flowed instead because one or the other of us was having problems coping with the debilitating and heartbreaking disease that had disrupted our once halfway-normal lives, she would listen, comfort, and then . . . tell another joke.

The jokes and stories continued well after the group had ended, over a glass of wine or on the phone, and we swiftly became part of each other's everyday life. Sometimes I wondered how was it that a middle-aged Jewish shoe saleswoman from New York and a young actress from Australia could even relate to one another, let alone become such close friends. But the bond between us was strong, and, oddly enough, the real learning took place in those challenging and confronting places of our polar-opposite personalities and lifestyles.

Margie could be both irritatingly bossy and ridiculously vain. I was a struggling actress with three jobs and no money to spend on fashion, yet she never failed to criticize my wardrobe, particularly my scuffed shoes. But the next time I saw her she'd be laden with armloads of expensive, perfect hand-me-downs. She told me I was beautiful in one breath and criticized my tousled, unkempt hair and lack of makeup in the next. However, a day later, she'd invite me to her house and introduce me to her "hair guy," Tony, who was instructed to "fix it," for which she gladly paid a significant amount of money.

In her own language, she was teaching me that I was worthy of better things; that my beauty was worthy of a second glance; that my voice was worthy of being heard. I observed Margie like a rare creature, taking mental notes about life and love. Watching Margie order an individualized salad taught me how to get what I want. Watching Margie meticulously accessorize her outfit and proudly do a turn in front of the mirror taught me how to appreciate my unique beauty. She embodied qualities that I craved in myself. Whether they were already there and just needed her encouragement, or whether it was she who instilled them, I could not be sure. However, I recognized and enjoyed her wisdom, and thus began writing my uniquely Margie lessons down—the way she delivered them—in a small booklet I liked to call Observations and Lessons for the Extraordinary Woman: Expressly for Emma Gordon and Other "Young Things," by Marjorie Myers.

LESSON ONE
These days, women under thirty don't carry umbrellas. Stupid. If it looks like rain, carry an umbrella; it'll save your hair.

LESSON TWO

Try on as many shoes as needed, with no guilt. Likewise, try on as many men as needed, with no guilt. However if foot is too wide for shoe, do not push. Alike, if woman is too wise for man, also do not push.

LESSON THREE

"Fake it until you make it." If you have absolutely no idea what to do, smile like this (Margie illustrates wide confident smile) and pretend. (Margie shrugs her narrow shoulders) "What, you think I knew how to sell shoes?"

LESSON FOUR

Speak up and be heard. Always. Have a voice regardless of what accent it comes in.

LESSON FIVE

Love . . . Love . . . Love! Give it a shot. You never know. Nobody's an expert. None of us know. Just give it a shot!

LESSON SIX

Always use a coaster. (Margie had a thing about water spots on good furniture, and proper guest behavior.)

LESSON SEVEN

Treat yourself to real clothes. You only live once. Your body deserves it. Wearing real fibers means that when your body sweats, it is actually crying in relief!

LESSON EIGHT

Share. Nothing is ever good alone. Share the goodness.

Cultivate friendships. Raise them, grow them, and nurture them, for they too are family.

For me, my friendship with Margie was unique and irreplaceable. However, if one were to attempt to concoct a similar relationship, you would need the following ingredients: one cup mother, one cup teacher, one cup friend. I am honored, in the truest sense of the word, that she invited me to be a part of her journey. Margie died on February 19, 2007. She approached dying as she did living—with laughter, courage, and the grace that defined her life. I had known Margie just shy of two years when she passed, and I remain painfully jealous of anyone who had the opportunity to know her longer. I am still struggling to conceive of—and live in—a world without the life force, the powerhouse, the firecracker that was Margie Myers.

Emma Gordon, a young Australian actress, has appeared in numerous New York and regional productions and is currently producing a short film and writing a play about her extraordinary Wednesday-night "Gilda Girls." Emma lives in Brooklyn, New York.

The Third Kind of Teacher

Leslie J. Wyatt

Some teachers possess a contagious enthusiasm that splashes onto those around them. Theirs is a true gift for inspiring students, leaving them thirsting for knowledge. Other teachers, those of unusual charisma or personality, seem to kindle fires in their pupils, enabling them to reach for academic heights and dreams they hadn't known were remotely possible.

Then there are the teachers whom we don't always notice or often appreciate until years later. They are the unsung heroes who rarely set the academic world abuzz. These are the third kind—the quiet, faithful, unassuming instructors whose simple patience and kindness make the world a brighter and safer place. They may remain in the background, but by their unique sensitivity and calm demeanors, they somehow help students stay afloat in a heedless sea of humanity.

Mr. Cameron was the third kind.

He wasn't one of those dashing young male teachers who set girls giggling during lunch break. In fact, to my eleven-year-old eyes, he wasn't handsome at all, really, and he was bordering on ancient—his brown hairs losing ground to the gray ones. At not much more than five feet six inches tall, no one would call him an impressive figure, and he probably liked that just fine. While I'd passed him in the hall many times, I was never sure he saw me. He always strode past with steps much longer than most people's, eyes intent on his destination.

I'd heard complaints from upper classmen: "Mr. Cameron makes you work way too hard." Or, "Mr. Cameron's class never does anything fun."

Academics came easily for me, but as an introvert with crooked teeth and cat's-eye glasses, I was barely treading water socially, and I never thought of school as fun. All I asked out of the experience was the chance to survive the school day without completely drowning.

Thus, I slipped into my classroom before the bell rang that first day of school, September 1970, and scooted behind a desk near the window and toward the front, where I hoped no one would realize that I came in all by myself and didn't have a friend excitedly holding a seat for me . . . or vice versa. I was so focused on reaching my little island of safety before the tsunami of the students flooded through the door, I didn't notice Mr. Cameron seated at his desk.

"Hello," he said, startling me.

I gulped and looked up. "Hi."

"I'm Mr. Cameron. Who might you be?"

"Leslie." My cheeks flushed to their usual hot, bright pink, and I stared down at my hands, longing for the floorboards to part and swallow me—desk and all. How dumb. I could have at least told him my last name, or smiled, or *something*!

"Pleased to meet you, Leslie."

I flicked my eyes up to meet his for the tiniest second, checking for any sign that he thought I was foolish. But there was none—just a smile and a fine and steady gaze before he looked back down at the book in front of him.

When the bell rang, the usual chaos ensued as students settled in their seats, and then came the relatively silent period during which we all waited to find out what kind of teacher we'd inherited this year. Mr. Cameron, his navy cardigan sweater laying neatly over a blue oxford shirt, took up what would become a familiar stance—leaning against the front of his desk, legs crossed, a book in one hand, a piece of chalk in the other. He had none of the false excitement other teachers staged on the first day of school. He simply introduced himself, took roll call, called us up one by one for our books—and that was that.

As week succeeded week, I found that in some ways the upperclassmen had been correct. Fifth grade was hard work under Mr. Cameron. He expected students to follow his directions to the letter, do their best work, and hand their homework in on time. He drew a firm line on whispering during class and loaded on extra work for those who did not heed his warning. However, he was also never too busy to help a student with a math or grammar concept, and no matter how many times it took for a child to understand, he was invariably patient in his explanations. No one dared tease another within his hearing, nor laugh at a less than stellar response to one of his questions.

"Can you believe old Cameron?" I overheard one boy say to another at recess.

"Yeah. Talk about a stick in the mud."

But when I looked at the short, upright figure patiently presiding over a game of foursquare, I suddenly knew I loved my teacher—and not in a puppy love, schoolgirl crush kind of way. I loved him in an appreciative, respectful, *I-admire-you-for-who-you-are* kind of way. His kindness, his patience, and his clear sense of justice won my heart.

From then on, I watched his every move and even took to walking like him—stretching my short legs as far as I could. I looked ludicrous, but I didn't think about that. My sole purpose was to emulate Mr. Cameron and hope that he would eventually notice that I, too, was purposeful and energetic. I always turned in neat, accurate homework, studied for quizzes, and typically did well because it was one thing I could do with relative ease. But my newfound admiration for, and desire to impress, Mr. Cameron inspired me to work harder than ever. I wanted to exceed his standards, hoping thereby to establish myself as a student worthy of his esteem.

Because he was the third kind of teacher, I don't think he ever knew I adored him or how fiercely and loyally my allegiance burned. Perhaps he only saw a shy, gangling girl eager to please, one who stood by him on the playground as often as not and who had a strange way of walking. He was so unassuming and humble. I'm sure he never suspected that it was his own kindness that had gained him that silent recess companion day after day.

Mr. Cameron never singled me out above any other student. He only gave me the grades I deserved, nothing better. He gave no indication I was any more special than the other twenty-four students in the room. But perhaps it was that very testament to his character—that each student was equally important to him, equally worthwhile and worthy of kindness and respect—that made me know I would miss him as I had missed no teacher before.

When the last day of fifth grade eventually came, I shyly offered and received one final smile, one final goodbye, and then walked, blinded by tears, through the hallways and out to the waiting school bus.

That was Mr. Cameron's last year of teaching at my school. I never again met him striding through the halls. A new teacher filled his desk and presided over the playground, and I moved forward to sixth grade and beyond. But all I have to do is close my eyes and to this day I see him—graying hair and cardigan sweater—as he looked at me that morning so long ago, and I feel warm affection and gratitude for this special teacher, whose kindness, fairness, and respect helped one certain child navigate the troubled waters of childhood.

Leslie J. Wyatt is a freelance writer for children and adults and has had more than ninety stories and articles accepted for publication. Among these works is her middle-grade historical novel *Poor Is Just a Starting Place* (released by Holiday House, Inc.). Leslie and her husband have been blessed with six children and enjoy life together in rural Missouri.

The Great and Powerful Zimmerman

Lauren Cassel Brownell

On a sweltering summer day in Room 304 of the Austin Community College campus, I came face-to-face for the first time with the Great and Powerful Zimmerman—ostensibly a meek and mild-mannered man whose power rested in the fact that he held my future in his hands. When he passed out the syllabus for Math 101—the one class that could prevent me from entering the college I desired—my heart began to race, my palms began to sweat, my stomach churned, and even my vision blurred. Every horrible experience I'd ever had with math (and there were many) passed before my eyes.

Always a straight-A student, in sixth grade, a failure to grasp math concepts led to my very first B, succeeded by a disappointingly predictable string of Cs and Ds. Finally, my sophomore year in high school, my math teacher, Mr. Harkins, called my parents in for a conference. "I'm sorry," he said, shaking his head and looking at the ground. "Lauren is simply incapable of learning advanced mathematical concepts. I don't think college is in her future; she'll never pass college-level math." My parents were stunned. I was broken hearted. At age fifteen, my boundless future had its first set of limitations placed upon it.

If I was fated to remain the math moron Mr. Harkins proclaimed me, I compensated by excelling in Advanced Placement English and honors science classes. I won statewide awards for my acting and debating skills and celebrated by avoiding math like the plague. I took—and barely passed—a remedial math course in order to be able to graduate from high school. And now, here I was face-to-face with Math 101, the dreaded college algebra class of my nightmares.

My goal was to limit my agony to six weeks instead of an entire semester. If I could pass the course, I could still squeak into the college of my choice. If I failed, I would have to settle for a college at the bottom of my list. And instead of being able to chart my own path for future success, I would have to search for a major, *any* major that did not require math. Mr. Harkins's words were still ringing in my ears.

In summer school, everything moved at lightning speed, so it only took three days for Mr. Zimmerman to recognize my ineptitude and ask me to stay after class. "What's going on, Lauren?" he asked. "You seem like a smart and capable young woman. But it's as if you aren't even trying."

Again, I stood before the Great and Powerful Zimmerman, reliving every painful mathematically induced moment I had ever experienced. Tears welled in my eyes. I looked up, met his steely gaze, and whispered, "I can't do math."

And he laughed! Thus far I hadn't even seen him crack a smile, but my heartrending confession caused him to laugh out loud. "Why would you say such a thing? Anyone can do math!"

"My tenth-grade math teacher called my parents in to tell us that I could not do math. He said I was hopeless, and that I'd never pass college-level math courses."

"Really?" The Great and Powerful Zimmerman's eyes flashed. "We'll just see about that. If you will come to my office every day and spend thirty minutes with me, I will prove that you not only can do math, you can excel at it." Even though I still believed Mr. Harkins and was convinced it would remain an exercise in futility, my future was at stake. I reluctantly agreed.

Because I had avoided any type of math for so long, our first several sessions were reviews of basic elementary algebra concepts, but his ability to explain them in a way my feeble math brain could understand helped me quickly progress. Before long, I was plodding through the exercises in my textbook solo. My mom would find me in my room late at night, working methodically through the review problems that Mr. Zimmerman assigned me. One day's work built on the next, and then the next. I began to see that there was no great math mystery, that—even when given the same clues as ordinary students—I did, indeed, have the ability to solve complicated algebraic problems.

Even when I caught up with my class, I continued my daily tutoring sessions with Mr. Zimmerman. Many times I would reach a point in a challenging problem where Mr. Harkins's words would echo in my head and threaten to squash my hard-won confidence. Luckily, Mr. Zimmerman always seemed to sense my pain, and when he did, he always said the same three words, problem after problem, assignment after assignment, day after day: "Trust *your* instincts."

With a great deal of reinforcement, hard work, and unrelenting faith, eventually the wise words of the Great and Powerful Zimmerman eradicated Mr. Harkins' false assumption. On the last day of class, as Mr. Zimmerman collected textbooks and had us fill out course evaluations, he called us to attention. "I've got one last announcement to make," he said. "Normally I don't make a practice of this, but because this student worked so hard, I think she deserves special recognition. The highest grade in the class on yesterday's final exam was received by our own Lauren Cassel."

I felt like I had won an Academy Award! Literally weeping with joy, I went up to give Mr. Zimmerman a hug.

"You had the ability to do it all along," he said, patting me dutifully on the back. "You, Ms. Cassel, have a talent for math."

Just as the Great and Powerful Oz opened the eyes of Dorothy and her pals to the qualities they had always possessed, the Great and Powerful Zimmerman opened my eyes to trusting *my* instincts, to listening to that voice that comes from inside and that says loudly and proudly, "I can!" He not only gave me the confidence to conquer Math 101, he gave me sage advice for conquering every challenge life throws my way.

And so, many miles further down the yellow brick road of my life, the girl who Mr. Harkins proclaimed would never be able to do math not only manages to balance her checkbook each month and help three children with math homework, she is also in charge of developing and managing multimillion dollar advertising and marketing budgets. And whenever she is asked to share a piece of advice with others, she thinks fondly of the Great and Powerful Zimmerman, smiles knowingly, and says, "Trust *your* instincts."

Lauren Cassel Brownell recently authored *Zen and the Art of Housekeeping*. Her work has also appeared in *Cup of Comfort for Women* and *Herstory*, as well as regional newspapers and magazines. She lives in Lubbock, Texas, with her husband and two children, where she is currently pursuing a master's degree in mental health counseling.

Mary Louise Winston's Protégé

Emily Tipton Williams

The summer before junior high school, my parents finally gave me my grandmother's violin. Holding the instrument for the first time, I was filled with awe and anticipation. I could hardly wait until the first day of school, until the day I could study violin in my junior high music class.

What a shock and disappointment.

Mary Louise Winston charged into the classroom like a dirt devil sweeping across the flat Texas prairie. "All right, straighten up!"

It was hard to believe the strong piercing voice bossing us around came from the tiny four-foot-ten-inch frame. Although impeccably dressed like a lady, complete with high heels and a matching purse, to me, Miss Winston was no lady—she was a taskmaster par excellence. She had eyes in the back of her head and X-ray vision, which could detect chewing gum hidden in a closed mouth. To a thirteen-year-old, she was the teacher from hell, not at all what I had imagined. For days all we did was tune our instruments and play scales.

By week's end, my angst was such that I confided in my parents.

"Perhaps you should change classes," my mother said.

"No! I love to play the violin."

"Then make the best of the situation."

As the weeks rolled by, I bowed my neck, learned my scales, and tried to separate the message from the messenger. It was difficult. At the time, mine was a shy personality. I jumped when the director's baton, which Miss Winston had converted to a lethal weapon, crashed into the conductor's stand to command attention. The baton was also used to single out individual offenders from within our orchestra who dared play a bad note. Picture us quivering with dread as she waggled the baton, repeatedly pointing toward each of us.

One hundred percent effort was demanded from each pupil. At times she would put her hands on her hips, stomp her foot and roar, "That's not good enough!" No one dared misbehave and risk an immediate trip to the principal's office.

The year passed slowly, and I was yet to be convinced Miss Winston was part of the human race. She drove her students unmercifully, it seemed to me. However, as my skills improved, the second year of junior high, I slowly developed an appreciation for Miss Winston. Nevertheless, it would be some years later before I realized how her precise and skilled teaching abilities effectively developed my musical talent.

I continued to play the violin through high school and college and graduated with a degree in music. I played in several symphony orchestras and became, you guessed it, a music teacher. As a new string teacher, I began to truly appreciate Mary Louise Winston and her unwavering penchant for discipline. I swiftly discovered, as a group, junior high students are perhaps the most difficult age to teach. They do not come imbued with discipline or precision. I found myself unconsciously reverting to teaching techniques used by Miss Winston.

After moving away from Fort Worth for a number of years, I returned with school-age children. My youngest daughter chose to play flute in middle school and, in a supreme act of déjà vu, her teacher was Miss Winston.

How fortunate to get a second chance to know Mary Louise Winston and learn about those things a student never knows. For instance, she never married because her fiancée was killed in World War II, and she never had children of her own. As a teacher, nothing gave her greater delight than her student's accomplishments. Her pupils consistently won awards at local and state competitions, and many went on to perform with symphony orchestras around the world. Once, we shared the stage together; she in a choir singing Handel's *Messiah* and I playing in the symphony orchestra. I hope it was as poignant for her as for me.

Emily Tipton Williams is a freelance writer, professional violinist, and retired music teacher. She serves as a lay minister in the Episcopal Church in Fort Worth, Texas. Emily's novel, *Restless Soul*, takes place in the United Kingdom, one of her frequent travel destinations. Emily and her husband, Mike, have five children and four grandchildren.

A Sparrow's Flight

Bhaswati Ghosh

My heart jumped in a zillion mismatched tango beats as I posted the article—a memoir piece on the bonding I shared with the radio during my growing up years—on the writing Web site I had just joined. This was my first brush with an online writing community, and I was still getting the hang of how it all worked.

Wading my way through the day's work at the office, I checked the forum for the umpteenth time to see if my essay had elicited any feedback. The tango beats froze for a moment when I saw a comment was posted by SJ, a Tennessee newspaper editor and leader of the nonfiction forum who had a sharp eye and never minced words in his critiques. I read the first few lines, "I went through your piece thrice, and there's little I found in it . . ." Fearing he was about to confirm my worst fears, I pulled back and gasped, and then paused, seeking courage to read farther. ". . . that needs changing. You have a great way with words and some interesting themes. If you haven't started selling your writing, I think you should start doing so right away."

Was I reading right? The man—known to be ironfisted when it came to compliments—had read my article three times and didn't feel it needed any change? Just to be sure, I read *his* comments thrice.

Shortly after SJ reviewed my essay, we began corresponding by posting notes on the writing forum's chat room. After a few exchanges, he adopted me as his "best Indian friend" and offered his writing support on an ongoing basis, which unleashed the scribbling bird inside me. He became the giant eagle that took this jittery sparrow under his wings.

One day, when we met again on the cyber highway—SJ in his morning at work, I in my evening after work—he asked if I had ever thought of visiting the United States. I told him I certainly had, and now more than ever, since I was acquiring many American friends. "But it's only a far-fetched dream," I replied, adding a cyber sigh. I didn't have the wherewithal to make this treasured-but-costly voyage.

"Well, just write a book and then use the contract money to buy your ticket," he responded, as matter-of-factly as ever.

I laughed so hard I imagined it flying over the Internet and coming through his speakers. "I can't write a book! I find it so daunting." I tapped the send key.

Typical of his optimism, he shot back. "You never know until you at least try, do you?"

As our editing relationship progressed, I realized that my eagle wasn't so taken with his sparrow that he would now shower me with unwarranted praise. Whenever he found my writing wanting, he did not spare me his scathing comments. If he felt a piece of writing didn't work, then it just didn't work, and he would invariably instruct me to "try again," or "flesh it out."

During this time, I continued to visit the writing forum. I loved interacting with other aspiring writers, but I was often perplexed by American lingo. My English skills were substantial, but the slew of slang expressions they used baffled me. When I confided to SJ that some forum members publicly teased my inability to understand colloquial American—when I took what they said literally, and they actually meant something completely different—he was livid. "Who made fun of you?" he quipped. "I'll whup them!"

He also vowed to teach me a new slang expression daily. And SJ took his job seriously. Every day, he asked me to take notes as he taught me phrases such as, "drop back and punt," "saved by the bell," "face the music," and many, many more. He would make up humorous stories to illustrate how Americans used the expressions, and when I received them, I would laugh aloud. In time, the list stretched beyond the pages of my small notebook so I bought a bigger one. Not only had SJ become my dictionary for interesting, weird, and funny new words, he had also become my facilitator for digging out the origins of these quirky phrases. The Tennessee eagle and the Indian sparrow laughed often and long.

Like the best of teachers, he seemed to sense when I needed support and reached into his compliment basket to send me an endless stream of encouraging words, such as "I am proud of you," or "You will do it," or "When you become a famous writer, I will tell the world I knew her when . . ." Every single time he said those heartening words, I knew he meant them.

On the other hand, my mentor also gave me moments of misery. A master procrastinator, he would take forever to reply to e-mails, even when I was desperately awaiting his critiques so I could meet a pressing deadline. He would promise repeatedly to send his feedback "soon," but "soon" turned into weeks and months. These occasions did ruffle my feathers, especially when I gave him the initial draft of the first chapters of my book.

My book represented the pinnacle of this mentor-disciple bond. I chose to write about American slang and colloquialisms, of course. It seemed wise to write a book based on my recent trials and tribulations. Initially, SJ was very supportive, but the pressure made us both impatient.

Since I was anxious to receive feedback, I would virtually demand that he make time for a special chat regarding the project. He agreed, but every time I expressed doubt or didn't like what he said, he flung a reply that was the virtual equivalent of a spanking. Our relationship now included occasional spats. When I asked him if I should include a specific number of slang expressions in the book, he snapped, "Nope. If you decide to include 500 and then get stuck on 498, you will freak."

I was furious. "No, I won't." I struggled to restrain my sense of outrage.

"Yes, you will," he reiterated, "I know you."

"Don't be so sure," I responded, jabbing the send button.

"If writing a book were that easy, everyone would be writing one."

"But I am (like) everyone, too," I retorted, worrying again that maybe I wasn't ready to write a book.

And then he flipped everything. "No, my little sparrow, you are not. You are a special one." And then, through every stage of writing the book, from pitching the proposal to editing the manuscript line by line, SJ remained my trusted mentor—an affectionate father figure at times, a strict and picky schoolmaster at others. From helping me expand the list of expressions, to dispatching truckloads of encouragement, to sternly pointing out areas that didn't work, he didn't rest until he had done everything possible to help me do my best.

When I finally received his critiques, SJ, the editor, seemed satisfied with the first four chapters. Once he read the draft of the fifth one, he changed his mind:

SJ: *This is the best chapter you've written so far.*
Me: *Really? Thanks.*
SJ: *But now your previous chapters won't work.*
Me (aghast): *Why? You said you liked them.*
SJ: *I did say that, but now you've set yourself a new standard by writing this one. You see, the other chapters must match this.*
Me: *Why do you have to make it so difficult for me?*
SJ: *I will always take you to higher summits.*

Until I reached the finish line and handed him the final manuscript, fully expecting it to be returned—once again—dotted with his red scribbles, he remained my most trusted writing friend and my most astute editor. His honest and discerning feedback became a vital catalyst for my growth as a writer—and author—and gave me the wings to expand far beyond my borders. To this day, the giant eagle continues to guide this partly dim-witted, mostly obedient sparrow from across the oceans.

Bhaswati Ghosh was born and educated in New Delhi. She worked for broadcast media, Web portals, educational organizations, and publishing houses before picking up her pen. Her work has been published in leading Indian dailies, U.S. magazines, the anthology *Letters to My Mother*, as well as Web sites and e-zines. *Making Out in America*, her first book-length work resulting from her brush with everyday Americanisms, is awaiting publication.

One Student at a Time

Wayne Scheer

I wore black long before Goth became a fad. Like some modern-day Goth teenagers, I had a penchant for despair and donned all-black clothing in the early sixties, when my youthful optimism collided with the Bay of Pigs and the Cuban Missile Crisis. The truth was I fell into a deep funk and coped by declaring a season of mourning for the "safe" world I had known, a world that seemed to be careening toward obliteration. I was also a skinny, shy kid who loved to hide in his room while furiously penning weird stories about a character I named Bluey Swanson, an aspiring superhero whose efforts to save the world destroyed him. I became increasingly convinced this was also my destiny.

My parents, particularly my stolid, regimented father, had no idea what to do with their rebellious and odd son. Up until then I had been an honor student, but by the end of my freshman year, thanks to my sense of despair, I failed most of my subjects. What was the point of finishing homework or preparing for a test when the world was going to end in a nuclear blast?

By my sophomore year, I was failing every subject except English, and that was solely because I lucked into having one unusual, life-changing teacher who engaged my curiosity. Miss Linkey was not only young, enthusiastic, and accepting, she celebrated independent thinking. And she was a bit of a rebel herself. When our high school principal discouraged anyone from reading *The Catcher in the Rye*, Miss Linkey devised a clever plan. After first selecting a small group of students she thought would benefit from private tutoring, holding her fingertips to her lips to keep it amongst ourselves, she told us that she was having a "secret" discussion group on Holden Caulfield. She even suggested that we pirate our copies of *The Catcher in the Rye* into the classroom by hiding them inside a hardcover copy of *A Tale of Two Cities*. If the principal came by, we would pretend to be discussing Dickens.

Around the same time, the guidance counselor called my parents to meet with my teachers and discuss my academic problems. My father had already decided that public school wasn't for me. He was convinced I needed discipline and had begun researching military schools. When he announced his decision, the counselor—and most of my teachers—nodded in agreement. My mother, however, between sobs, begged me to promise to try harder in school. I suddenly identified completely with Holden Caulfield being told to "buckle down," and blithely shrugged, which I hoped would fully articulate my disdain for almost everything.

Suddenly, Miss Linkey cleared her throat. "I don't think we should give up," she said, facing the school counselor and his band of brothers. "Why don't you give me till the end of the term? If he isn't passing all his courses with at least Bs, I will personally help you select and enroll him in the toughest military school we can find." Relieved, my mother leapt to her feet and hugged Miss Linkey. I had never seen anyone hug a teacher before.

My father grunted. "You must think you're some kind of miracle worker," he said. "Wayne's lazy. What he needs is for someone to stick a rod up his keister."

Miss Linkey stood up, towering over me. "I can do that if I have to," she said. "But I would rather light a fire under him. Wayne is a talented writer. He just hasn't felt sufficiently motivated."

"Motivated, huh?" My father crossed his arms and glowered.

"Please," Miss Linkey said, pausing. "There is no point in having him start a new school in the middle of the year. If he hasn't turned things around by the fall, then . . ."

"Okay," my father conceded, "But if he doesn't pass all his classes, we won't have this discussion again. He'll be in military school where he belongs."

Miss Linkey smiled broadly. "Don't worry. He'll not only pass; he'll earn Bs or better."

My father scowled. "I'll settle for Cs."

"I won't," Miss Linkey said, turning to look straight at me. The intensity in her eyes nailed me to my seat. I didn't speak, smile, or shrug.

The next day Miss Linkey marched into my homeroom and asked if she could speak to me privately. Once we were alone in the hallway, she turned to face me. "You owe me, Wayne," she said, pausing briefly. "*Big* time." Part of me wanted to retreat behind my rebellious nonchalance, but her dynamic personality and bravado had gotten under my skin.

And the woman proved relentless. Our book discussions moved from Salinger to Fitzgerald's *The Great Gatsby* to Updike's *Rabbit, Run* to Thoreau's *Civil Disobedience* to Kerouac's *On the Road* to Twain's *The Adventures of Huckleberry Finn*. They were invigorating, and when over, Miss Linkey extracted a price—I was required to stay behind so she could tutor me.

Sometimes I silently completed my homework assignments, and sometimes we discussed American history or world geography in depth. Miss Linkey admitted that she didn't remember much algebra, so we put our heads together until we solved the equations and finished all of my assignments. She may not have known much about algebra, but she was fluent in Spanish. While I struggled to recite simple phrases like "*¿Hola, Juan, donde es la playa?*" she often read *Don Quixote* aloud—in lilting Spanish—which lured me deeper into the world of literature. Not content to have me simply complete my regular assignments, Miss Linkey created additional science or history homework and told me I couldn't come to the book discussion until they were completed. Miss Linkey was tough, but she definitely lit a fire under me.

By the end of the term, I hadn't quite fulfilled Miss Linkey's promise to my father. No matter how hard I had tried, I couldn't get above a C-plus in algebra, but I did earn solid As in history, Spanish, and science, and an A-plus in English. When Miss Linkey called my father to apologize for the low math grade, my father was so pleased he didn't grumble and happily agreed to let me stay in public school.

The next year, I was back in public school sporting a new wardrobe consisting of rumpled chinos and turtlenecks, albeit black ones. Even though the Cuban Missile Crisis had subsided and Castro stopped aiming missiles toward our shores, I still held doubts that our deteriorating civilization would survive, but I restricted my defiance to practically worshipping Beat poetry.

Even though I would have been willing to continue our tutorials, Miss Linkey made it clear I didn't need her anymore. She did, however, continue to "assign" long, personalized reading lists. She also read everything I wrote and always had positive things to say, even when the work was clearly substandard. Not only was Miss Linkey's faith in me unshakable, her standards had somehow become my standards—her enthusiasm and commitment to learning had seeped into my consciousness.

Many, many years later, when I returned to my old high school for a reunion, Miss Linkey had long ago retired, but her legend lived on. In fact, when sharing stories about her, one of the English teachers mentioned that Miss Linkey had always chosen one problem student each year. One year it was a boy, and the next a girl, and each student was invited to her special book discussions, and each received special tutoring and a tailored reading list.

"Were you one of her students?" the teacher asked, noticing, perhaps, the surprised look on my face.

"Yes," I said, fondly remembering the many days I had spent under Miss Linkey's tutelage. "Everyone else was ready to ship me off to military school until she begged my parents for one last chance to get my head on straight."

"I'll bet you didn't know that she taught at a military academy before coming here." His eyes danced mischievously.

I laughed aloud, and then raised my glass for a toast. "Miss Linkey, I salute you!"

Wayne Scheer retired after teaching writing and literature in college for twenty-five years. He then followed his own advice and began writing. He's published both fiction and nonfiction and has been nominated for a Pushcart Prize and a Best of the Net. Wayne lives with his wife in Atlanta, Georgia.

Milkshakes and Shoelaces

Linda Pischke

"O bee-u-tiful for spaa-cious skies." The voice of our third-grade teacher filled the classroom as she strolled up and down the aisles between our wooden desks, her high heels clicking on the tile floor. She paused to look over a student's shoulder. "Well done, Marsha. Well done," she said to her star pupil.

"Thank you, teacher," Marsha replied.

Mrs. Visovotti resumed singing, even as she leaned down to place her hand over Karen's. "That 't' goes all the way to the top line, like this. That's it. Good, very good."

Writing class in Mrs. Visovotti's third grade was not just a lesson in penmanship. It was history, patriotism, and music all rolled into one. Every afternoon at precisely two o'clock, we opened our dark-blue workbooks with the solid and dotted lines. Then we sharpened number two pencils and began the task of copying the patriotic songs that had been perfectly transcribed on blackboard chalk lines. Immersed in the historical words of *America the Beautiful, The Star-Spangled Banner, Battle Hymn of the Republic,* and other ballads now lost to my memory, we were expected to write every verse of every song, then memorize the words and sing them together.

The year was 1954. I was nine years old and excited to be in the third grade. My family was part of the post-war migration from city to suburbs, when rows of houses sprouted up in the middle of farm fields, causing the rapid expansion of former one-room schools like Woodside Elementary in Brookfield, Wisconsin. It was a time for heroes and heroines, a time when children dreamed of riding off into the sunset with Roy Rogers and Dale Evans. Even then I recognized that Mrs. Visovotti was no ordinary teacher.

She looked as old as my grandmother with silver hair twisted into a knot at the top of her head. I remember tailored suits with matching neck scarves and clip-on earrings and a wrinkled face accented with pink rouged cheeks. But Mrs. Visovotti had the energy of a much younger woman. She fluttered around the room, her high-pitched voice excited with the possibilities of everything we could learn. And the most wonderful memory of all was how she made every child feel very special.

"America! America!" her voice rose in a crescendo then stopped abruptly.

"Leroy," she said shaking her head. "You must hold the pencil as I have instructed you. And please don't rest your head on the desk."

Leroy Cotter straightened himself, and placed his chin on his hand. He was the poor boy in our class. Everyone knew that. Leroy had a dirty face and sad blue eyes that stared out from under a mop of unruly blond hair. His shoes made a *flop, flop* sound because the laces were missing, and he had the annoying habit of holding on to his trousers and hitching them up as he walked. One morning, Mrs. Visovotti brought him a pair of shoelaces. Then she took a piece of clothesline, slipped it through the belt loops on Leroy's pants, and tied it securely so they wouldn't fall down.

When Leroy didn't finish his homework, Mrs. Visovotti appointed one of the smart girls to show him how. They would sit at the back of the room, Leroy and Marsha or sometimes Cheryl, going over lessons taught the day before while Mrs. Visovotti patiently hovered nearby saying, "Well done, well done."

Everybody talked.

"Leroy smells," they would say.

"Yeah, I bet his house smells too," I said. "Did you know he has nine brothers and sisters?"

"Poor people shouldn't have so many kids," said Claudia.

I considered myself an authority on Leroy's situation. He lived at the end of our street in an old farmhouse weathered down to the bare boards. The porch was rotted off and tall weeds grew where the barn and outbuildings once stood. A two-lane highway separated our new subdivision and the acres of abandoned fields around the Cotter home. It was the road I walked to school with Leroy—well, not exactly *with* Leroy.

He walked on the other side, head down, kicking at stones along the way.

So I informed the other kids that Mr. and Mrs. Cotter spent their evenings at Rita's Bar and Grill. I knew this because my grandpa saw them there.

No one really liked Leroy, no one except Mrs. Visovotti. She loved him just like she loved everyone else. And without a word of criticism for our attitudes or sermons about how we should behave, she taught us to love him, too.

Leroy's head was back on his desk, and he was breathing heavily in sleep.

Mrs. Visovotti touched his shoulder. "Are you tired, dear?" she whispered.

"Yes ma'am," he said sitting up again. "I sure am."

"Did you stay up too late last night?"

"No ma'am. I didn't go to sleep at all."

"Why on Earth not?"

"I was watching the babies, ma'am."

"Why were you watching the babies?"

"It was my turn, ma'am. If we don't keep them rats out of their beds, they bites 'em."

"I see," said Mrs. Visovotti calmly. She took a deep breath. "Did you drink the milkshake I brought you this morning, Leroy? It's very nutritious."

"Yes ma'am. Thank you. It was good."

Mrs. Visovotti turned and walked to the front of the room. With her back to us, she began to sing again, her voice hushed in a lullaby.

At the end of third grade, the Cotter family moved out of the farmhouse. No one paid much attention. No one cared. When they tore the old house down, my father said the structure was so dilapidated the workmen reported finding over a hundred pounds of wild honey in the walls. Neighborhood gossip died with the fading memories, and I didn't think about Leroy any more.

Fifteen years later, at the wedding of a friend, I was introduced to a well-groomed young man in a gray suit and tie with blonde hair and incredible blue eyes. He looked straight at me and smiled.

Very handsome, I thought.

"Do you remember Leroy?" my friend asked.

"Indeed, I do." I said extending my hand.

Well done, Mrs. Visovotti! Well done!

Linda Pischke works full-time as a nursing-home social worker and volunteers as a group facilitator at a local county jail. Her published works include two reference books, and articles in *The Catholic Herald* and *The National Catholic Reporter*. She is currently working on a collection of personal stories by women prisoners.

Reversal of Fortune

Valerie Schultz

"Twenty-five times today he called me this name," Ricardo said, pacing. "I felt like I was getting ready to . . . to . . ." He popped his right fist hard into his left palm, so that we had no doubts about what he felt like doing to his tormentor. The other six inmates nodded their heads in agreement. Some of them had overheard the insults, and most knew exactly how it felt when you were about to do something you knew you would regret.

"You know what, though?" Ricardo continued. "While I was listening to him and getting madder, I also had this feeling of peace—this feeling that God was inside me. And I felt okay, you know, calm." Ricardo turned to look at me, as though confident I would understand this feeling. And I did. But I didn't have that feeling anywhere near as frequently as he assumed I did. Although

I volunteered to facilitate a spiritual sharing group in the state prison, I didn't do so because I felt holy in any way. While I was a nice, well-mannered mother, I had not achieved the level of spiritual evolvement they seemed to imagine.

Ricardo's feeling of peace and acceptance was hard won and hard to hold. What he didn't know was that peace remained as fleeting in my life as it did in his—maybe even more so. Ricardo was learning to live a life of faith under hazardous circumstances, within confining walls, facing situations in which he was constantly tested, constantly scrutinized, often challenged, and sometimes threatened. I had the luxury of being able to leave. I could go home and take a holiday from working so hard to live up to a new code. I could let my guard down. He couldn't.

When I first volunteered for this program, I thought that I would be the wise teacher and that they—those poor captive men—would be the students. The opposite was true. I gained far more than I gave. My "students" thought I was sacrificing my precious time for them, giving up much more meaningful and pleasurable activities to hang out with them, but really my sessions with them became some of the most spiritually fulfilling hours of my week. When I told them I thought of them as my other parish, they smiled and shook their heads, as if they didn't believe me. When I told them that coming to the prison to be with them enriched my life, they scoffed; they wouldn't be caught dead there if they didn't have to serve their time.

The less I talked, the more we all learned—from each other. Just as Ricardo taught us about patience, Michael shared a lesson on humility. "Before I was convicted, I was in control," he said. "I had my own company; my employees and my family obeyed me. I was the boss; I gave the orders. But here, here I take orders." And we watched him come to terms with his utter lack of control. Michael believed that he would be a humbler, less-controlling man when he finally returned to the outside. He taught us to reconsider our proud and headstrong ways, the behaviors that lead only to trouble, and sometimes to prison.

In this most unspiritual of places, I met people in the most astonishing grips of metanoia—that radical change of heart to which we are all called. I watched them pray right down to their guts, right down to their naked souls. I marveled at their commitment to reading and discussing the Bible, the catechism, and whatever spiritual writings they could get their hands on. I watched them labor, day after day, to live those teachings. I saw some very brave souls dare to attempt community outreach within the walls of the state prison. These once-hardened men reached out to others who were in pain, who needed a kind word, who were confused or frightened—which, in a prison setting, is a very brave, selfless thing to do. Most inmates just want to do their time, keep their heads down, stay out of trouble, and count the days until they are released. Few give any thought to making prison a better place for others.

But some do.

Valerie Schultz's essays and short fiction have appeared in the *Los Angeles Times*, the *Chicago Tribune*, and *High Plains Literary Review*, as well as numerous Catholic and parenting publications. She is a weekly columnist for the *Bakersfield Californian* and a guest columnist for *America*.

American Girl

Renie Burghardt

I was fourteen when my grandparents and I immigrated to America in 1952. My grandparents had raised me. We had not only lived through the ravages of World War II in our native Hungary, we had survived four years in a refugee camp in Austria. We entered the United States as displaced persons (DPs) with high hopes of becoming Americans.

We landed in Cleveland, Ohio, where our sponsor had jobs waiting for my grandparents. Although they had little money, my grandparents enrolled me in an all-girls Catholic school taught by nuns. To a mousy, shy, displaced girl, American girls looked both rich and beautiful. Many of the older girls drove big cars to school, something I couldn't even imagine was possible. I envied their confidence, their swinging ponytails, their distinctly American bobby socks, and their carefree, fun-loving ways. I longed to look like them, but I not only looked different, I had a thick accent. And I had a traumatic past that still haunted me. Every time I entered that school, I did so with great trepidation, painfully aware of being different.

By the time June came around, I had been in my new school for five months, yet I remained shy and mousy and barely noticed by the other girls. I spent my first summer in America working at a local dime store and hanging out with immigrant friends in ethnic neighborhood establishments.

Summer ended much too soon, and when it was time to don my blue-and-gold jumper and white blouse, I felt that familiar sense of dread. Although some of the girls greeted me cheerily, I had not magically transformed into an American swan over the summer, something they all noticed and something that remained painfully obvious to me. But then I walked into Sister Mary Anne's sophomore English class, and soon everything changed for me.

Sister Mary Anne had twinkling blue eyes, a kind face, a smile that lit up the classroom, and a gentle, understanding manner. Although I said nothing, she seemed to instantly recognize my pain and began gently asking me questions about my life in front of the class. "Renie has a fascinating story to tell," she said, addressing the class. "She has lived a life that we cannot even imagine, and I hope she will tell us more about it so that we can understand just a bit how it felt to be in her shoes." She may have looked like an ordinary nun to those

American girls, but to me she looked like a radiant angel—my own guardian angel!

As such, my angel promptly paved a way for me to become part of the group. "Girls, please pause to think about all that Renie has gone through. Be kind and helpful to her, so she can feel more at home here. Make her happy to be here, to be one of you now. Ask her your own questions, and listen not only with your ears but with your heart."

At the end of class that day, she announced our first assignment. "I want each of you to write an essay of four or five pages about something remarkable that has happened to you." Although I wasn't certain what writing an essay entailed, I knew that she was giving me an opportunity to write about my past, a chance to finally introduce myself to my American classmates.

I put my heart and soul into writing about what it was like being crammed onto a ship with hundreds of hopeful refugees on our way to a new country. I wrote about the young American boy who worked on the ship, and the day he brought me my first Coca Cola. I wrote about how it felt when I first saw the Statue of Liberty, how its symbolism thrilled me, as if it were welcoming me personally to America. I wrote about how it felt waiting to be processed at New York Harbor, half afraid that they wouldn't let us in, and how it felt to be far away from home, in a new country where the language and customs were vastly different. I poured out all my feelings, including that of being an outsider, and with each word I wrote, I realized that writing provided a way to release all those feelings of being an outsider. It also provided a way to reconnect to myself and to others.

The day after we handed in our essays, Sister Mary Anne asked me to read mine to the entire class. I remember that slow walk to the front of the class, taking the essay in my hands and beginning very nervously. I remember feeling afraid that the beautiful American girls would be repelled by my accent and everything that had happened in my life, but as I continued to read, albeit slowly, I noticed that they were all leaning forward in their seats, paying close attention to my every word. When I reached the end, I kept my head down until I heard my class-mates applauding!

Later, in the hallway, girls who had never spoken to me before approached me to tell me how much they liked my essay. And one girl told me about a popular magazine called *American Girl* and even suggested that I send the story to their "By You" section. It was accepted for publication, and the magazine paid me a whopping $10 for it! With the stroke of my pen, I began the real transition from being a "displaced person" to an American girl.

When I brought the published essay to Sister Mary Anne, she was elated. "You are a real writer, Renie, and I am so proud of you!" And all during that year and the remaining two years, whenever I had a problem, or didn't understand something, I always turned to Sister Mary Anne. She was my ally, my men-tor, and my biggest fan. But she was that to all the girls—we all loved her.

Two years later, when I tossed my cap in the air as a member of the graduating class of 1955, I thought about Sister Mary Anne. I remembered her kind eyes and her gentle manner, but most of all I remembered how she took the hand of a shy, reticent girl and introduced her to her new world. Because of her, I felt safe enough to conquer the culture shock that held me back, and to open up to my classmates. Because of Sister Mary Anne, I went on to graduate as the confident young American girl I had longed to become. And to that gentle teacher in the blue-and-white habit, I will be eternally grateful.

Renie Burghardt is a freelance writer who was born in Hungary. She has been published in over sixty anthologies and many magazines. She lives in the country and loves nature, animals, reading, hiking, and spending time with family and friends.

A Life Born of Ink, Clay, Twigs, Mirrors, and Ribbons

Judith Campbell

Among the first things I noticed about school in Hyde Park, Massachusetts, was that the desks and chairs were bolted to the floor; that each desk had a thick glass inkwell in the right-hand corner; and that the desktops bore the marks and memories of the generations of school children before me. To this day I can still remember the smell of linseed oil the custodian used on the wooden floors, the powdery smell of chalk dust, the waxy scent of newly opened, oversized Crayola crayons, and, weaving it all together, Miss Cunningham's rose perfume.

My first-grade teacher was a tall, slender woman with endless patience and a soothing voice. I adored her flowing skirts and the high-heeled shoes that announced her coming up behind me. This happened regularly because, on most days, I finished my assignment and kept myself out of her hair—and everyone else's—by writing stories on math paper which I'd folded into squares, and then drawing pictures to illustrate them, and she'd come over to investigate what I was doing.

Another teacher might have snatched the paper and the crayons and doled out mindless busy work to keep me quiet. But Mrs. Cunningham encouraged me to let my fledgling creative juices flow, as if she knew I needed a way to voice to my secret thoughts—mostly about a fantasy family—on tightly folded pieces of dun-colored paper.

Sometimes she'd come over and sit down on a low chair beside me and read my stories and look at my pictures and tell me how much she liked what I was doing. Once she even mounted one of my picture stories on a piece of bright-blue construction paper and put it up on the wall for the rest of the kids to see.

Unfortunately, unlike my first blissful year, in second and third grade, I spent a lot of time in "naughty" corners, but I still managed to learn subtraction, multiplication, and the shaky beginnings of the Palmer Method of penmanship. But neither of those teachers had Miss Cunningham's grace or sensitivity. They did not allow me to write any stories or draw any pictures other than those assigned. And somewhere during those two years, my parents got a divorce.

When I was promoted to the fourth grade, I had the incredible good fortune to have Miss Cunningham for a second time. She introduced me to ink pens and cursive writing, which I loved. The "good kids" got to go around once a week with a tin ink-pitcher and fill the inkwells. They were the ink monitors.

Miss Cunningham assigned me two of her more active monitorships: I clapped the erasers and went to the office for messages. As always, rather than squashing my energy, she found clever and useful ways to engage it, which ultimately taught me how to productively channel it for myself.

She also introduced me to grey, greasy, oily-smelling plasticene that we stored in hard balls in square, covered tins. We had to warm it up in our hands and work it with our fingers before we could get it soft enough to make anything. I loved that part so much my hands invariably smelled like it for days afterward. It also stuck to my shoes and stained my clothes where I'd sat on it, but, to me, clay was heavenly.

Once again, Miss Cunningham allowed me to express my budding creativity. She set up a table for me in a far corner, and the minute my class work was done, I made a beeline for the clay tins. Over the course of many weeks, contentedly off by myself, I quietly constructed a village of pretty houses and happy people, along with dogs and cats. I collected twigs and turned them into trees with tiny clay leaves; I filled gardens with pinhead-sized flowers; and in the center of my village, I decorated a skating pond fashioned from a hand mirror Miss Cunningham donated.

When she noticed my clay village rapidly expanding, Miss Cunningham brought in a large square of plywood and helped me shift the village onto it. When I ran out of space and couldn't think of anything else to add, Miss Cunningham stood silently beside me for several long minutes before turning to face me. "Oh, Judith, you really are an artist, aren't you?"

Her eyes sparkled and, with my permission, she displayed my village in the school foyer.

One day in early May, Miss Cunningham handed me a note to take home. "I'd like your mother to come in for a chat," she said, but gave me no clue why. I worried all weekend that my mother would be angry, but of course we didn't discuss it. My mother rarely went out any more, so when she showed up that Monday after school, more carefully dressed than she had been in some time, my hopes fluttered briefly, and then I quivered once again: *What had I done?*

Miss Cunningham walked us back out into the hallway where my clay village was still on display. "You have a very talented daughter, and I hope you don't mind, but I took the liberty of entering Judith's village in a children's art show competition . . . and I have exciting news." Miss Cunningham held up a brightly colored ribbon. "She won an honorable mention!"

I looked at my teacher, and then at my mother and asked, "What's an honorable mention?"

My mother and my teacher exchanged a glance. "Well," said Miss Cunningham, bending down to look into my eyes, "It's an award for a work of art that's very, very good. If it had been up to me, I would have given you first prize, but everything else in the show was either a painting or a drawing. Your sculpture was in a class all its own." She grinned, stood straight again, and turned to my mother. "And I have another surprise! She also won a scholarship to an ongoing children's art class at the Museum of Fine Arts in Boston. I know it might be a hardship, but I hope you'll find a way for her to attend."

My mother gasped, and then looked down at me and smiled. I hadn't seen her happy smile in a long time. Miss Cunningham reached out to squeeze my mother's hand.

And that summer, my mother not only made sure I went to the museum for my art class, on good days, we even stopped for ice cream on the way home.

The Rev. Dr. Judith Campbell is a Unitarian Universalist minister and retired professor of art. She authored two books on watercolor painting (F&W publishers and Appalachian Mountain Club Press), two volumes of poetry, and a number of poems and children's stories (Skinner House, a subsidiary of Beacon Press and other religious publications). She lives on Martha's Vineyard with her husband Chris and two creative felines.

An Indomitable Spirit

Roxanne Werner

When I was seven and broke my arm, a surgeon pieced it
together with steel pins and wrapped it in a cast. Something
else broke that year, something invisible and harder to heal. The
precise moment when my spirit fractured wasn't as
easy to identify—no X ray could locate a break—but
when it received the blows that created the wound,
the pain felt just as real.

I began second grade feeling burdened
to perform and wounded. Every day the
teacher wrote a task for us to complete
before lessons began on the board. The next
day, she added another, and each day I fell
short. The list grew longer and longer, and evidence of my shortcomings mounted. No matter
how hard I tried, I couldn't complete the tasks
on time; the cast weighed down my arm like

an anchor. Because I didn't work fast enough, I had to stay in during recess. I resented watching my classmates file out of the room and felt envious as they laughed and raced around the playground while I felt chained to my desk.

After my arm healed, I discovered another problem. Somewhere between my eyes and my brain letters did the dyslexic shuffle—*felt* became *left*, *from* became *form*; *there* became *three*. Words transformed before my eyes, making nonsense of sentences. I had to reread passages over and over until I puzzled them out. When my teacher placed an egg timer on my desk to make me work faster, my classmates pointed and whispered the words "dumb" and "stupid." I began to believe them and took out my frustration and anger on my crayons. The pencil box became a coffin for my self-esteem. Crumbled crayons lay buried under a pile of shredded wrappers.

One night my mother suggested I try Tae Kwon Do. I looked at my stick arms and legs. *Is she kidding?* I thought. *Something else to fail.* But mother could be formidable, so the next day, after school, we drove to the martial arts center.

The ex-marine who taught Tae Kwon Do had the booming voice of a drill sergeant—I heard Mr. Mullen before I saw him. His commands echoed above me as I climbed the flight of stairs. I hesitated at the top, opened the door a crack, and peered inside. Boys and girls of all ages stood in rows kicking. A short compact man dressed in a black uniform walked up and down the ranks correcting them.

"Come in," he said, without turning around. "Take off your shoes." Startled, I walked in and sat down on the floor to remove them. As I quickly learned, Mr. Mullen had eyes in the back of his head. Even when drilling, he was constantly aware of what every student in his class was doing. If I goofed off while he had his back to me, busily talking to a parent or another student, he knew. He had a sixth sense that told him exactly what each of us was doing at all times.

Mr. Mullen, or Sir, as we called him, ran a strict class. He demanded respect not only for himself but also for our classmates. "No matter how clumsy or awkward one of my students—your comrades—might be, no one will laugh or snigger," he commanded. "I expect *your* best, not *the* best." But he made it clear that didn't mean anyone could slack off—the man pushed us hard. Sir had a keen eye and assessed everyone's capabilities; he sized up mine better than I had ever done.

He proved tough but fair, and I soon found myself wanting to please him. Even when I dropped my guard and foolishly goofed around during class, I never resented dropping and doing push ups—the punishment was deserved. Although I wasn't the best athlete, I thrived in his class. I looked forward to the challenges and goals he set. I worked hard to live up to his trust in my abilities.

Week after week, while we practiced kicks and patterns, Sir talked to us. Without recognizing his full intention, I was learning much more than Tae Kwon Do. "Martial arts is a way of life, a code of honor, a set of ideals to be applied to more than the physical," Sir counseled, often clapping his hands together to emphasize "life," "honor," and "ideals." While we exercised and strengthened our bodies, his lectures worked their magic on our characters and our minds. "Cultivate an indomitable spirit," he said often, his blue eyes boring into mine. I always looked away, afraid his measuring gaze read the secrets hidden in my crayon box.

One afternoon he asked the class to line up in two long rows facing each other. He told us to drop into a horse stance. I stood opposite Chris, who had survived and overcome heart surgery and also needed to restore faith in her own abilities. We planted our feet shoulder-width apart and bent our knees lowering our bodies as though to sit on imaginary chairs. Sir walked up and down the line until he was sure everyone was in the proper stance. "Stop when you need to," he said, then turned to talk to another instructor, leaving us on our own.

A few students sat as soon as he turned away. Sir made no comment. It was up to us. There was no punishment, or reward, only our own choices. In a few minutes, my thigh muscles began to burn. Out of the corner of my eye I saw other students drop and sit on the floor. My eyes met Chris's; our gazes locked. I knew neither one of us was going to quit. Sweat beaded on my forehead and trickled down my back. My legs began to tremble. Breathing deeply, I clung to Sir's words, *indomitable spirit,* like a life preserver. One by one, the other students collapsed to the floor. They talked quietly, but as time passed they turned to focus on me and Chris, frozen in our stances. Just when I felt I couldn't hold the stance a second longer, Sir told Chris and me to sit down. Cheers and claps erupted from our classmates. Embarrassed, I ducked my head, but not before I saw Sir nod at me, a smile playing on his lips. My legs ached, but my heart soared.

School did not magically become easier after that. Words still scrambled, and bullies continued to call me dumb. But I didn't listen to them anymore. Like the surgeon who had repaired my arm, Mr. Mullen had placed steel pins in my broken spirit. When he wrapped a black belt around my waist five years later, the healing was complete. Sir helped me boldly face my demons and win. I wasn't a failure or a quitter. I had an indomitable spirit. I would always do *my* best.

Roxanne Werner is a freelance children's writer. When not writing, she can be found reading, gardening, bird-watching with her two cats, or dusting her son's Tae Kwon Do trophies. She lives with her family in New York State.

Tough Teacher Taught Tenaciously

Tanya J. Tyler

When it comes to tough teachers, I'll pit my sixth-grade teacher, Thelma Teasdale, against any other teacher on the planet. To give you a clue, we nicknamed her "Bulldog." Not that anyone dared to use that moniker in her presence; the consequences would have been traumatic.

Mrs. Teasdale was short and squat, like a bulldog. She wore her hair in a severe schoolmarm bun and glared at us through thick black-framed glasses. Her gravelly voice always seemed to be at maximum volume. "Stop slouching!" she snapped at students slumped in their seats. "Wrong answer!" she growled as we did math problems at the blackboard. "Do it over!" She constantly cracked an invisible whip over our heads.

But my classmates and I needed a whip occasionally. We were Class 6-1, which ostensibly meant we were the brightest students in all of PS 21 in the Bronx, New York. In the late 1960s, our neighborhood was populated by first- and second-generation Americans and African American families, like mine, that had "moved on up" from Harlem but were still struggling. We faced lowered expectations and skepticism about our ability to succeed.

But Mrs. Teasdale wouldn't let us use our economic situation as an excuse for not doing our best. She expected us to transcend the barriers society imposed on us. If we complained about the plentiful homework she gave us, she said, "Do it—or else!" Working on a report about various countries, some students copied directly from the encyclopedia. "That's plagiarism!" Mrs. Teasdale said. "Write it all over in your *own* words!" That was probably the worse thing about Mrs. Teasdale—we couldn't put anything past her. She was too sharp.

She insisted we come to school an hour before all the other students and stay an extra hour after school—every day for months—to study for the entrance exams to Hunter Junior High School for girls and Mount St. Michael Academy for boys, two prestigious New York City schools. "You're going to make them sit up and take notice when they see your test scores," she said. And she cracked the whip over our heads even more.

Mrs. Teasdale demanded the utmost deportment and decorum from us, in school and out. She issued an unbreakable "golden rule" that her male and female students could not "fraternize." She had seen some of us chasing each other. "From now on, the boys will walk home with the boys and the girls will walk home with the girls," she decreed. Having recently flirted with romance with one of the boys in my class, I longed to breach the code. But I wasn't brave enough to even consider going against the Bulldog's rules. I spent most of my time desperately trying not to cross Mrs. Teasdale, keeping a low profile in hopes of avoiding her wrath. I wasn't always successful.

A simple trip to the library is forever burned into my memory. When we returned to our classroom and flopped down at our desks, Mrs. Teasdale began grilling everyone about whether they had disobeyed her specific order not to talk in the library. I'd merely whispered a few words, which hardly qualified as a punishable offense, to my mind. When she directed her inquisition to me, I looked down and murmured, "I don't know."

The words were barely out of my mouth before Mrs. Teasdale shouted, "Stand up, Tanya! I know you were talking!"

I surged to my feet, seething, biting my lip to avoid shouting back, "Yeah, I *was* talking! So what are you gonna do about it, you big fat bulldog?" But no one was that foolish even when unjustly accused.

Mrs. Teasdale had a singular way of administering punishment. Instead of having us write a simple line, such as "I will not talk in the library," a hundred times, she created a fifty-word *paragraph*, entitled "Behavior," that we had to recreate neatly on lined paper at home—and have our parents sign, so they knew we'd misbehaved in school. I don't remember what it said, but I do remember when I had to write it twenty-five times.

One time, three classmates and I were supposed to meet Mrs. Teasdale in the school cafeteria to rehearse a song for our spring musical. We waited for what seemed an exceptionally long time, particularly for the always-prompt Mrs. Teasdale. We decided to go upstairs to see if she was in our classroom. She wasn't, so we raced each other back to the cafeteria, laughing and jumping the stairs two and three at a time. We burst around the last corner and started down the final flight of stairs. And there stood Mrs. Teasdale, blocking our path. The four of us froze in our tracks. She didn't yell. She just pointed at each of us in turn and said, "Behavior, Behavior, Behavior, and Behavior."

In all fairness, Mrs. Teasdale also provided enjoyable experiences. She took us on field trips to Albany, where we met our state senator, and to the Statue of Liberty. I remember we stood on the ferry singing, "Give me your tired, your poor, your huddled masses yearning to breathe free"—a song she'd taught us. For a project involving experiments with sound, she helped us build a xylophone out of wood scraps and used empty soda bottles we collected to teach us about musical tones. She helped us create a hallway display about our summer vacations. A world traveler herself—she'd been to India and Egypt, among other places—she wanted to open the world to us. It was, again, her way of showing us anything was possible if we worked hard. She never yelled at us when we were doing something creative. She was most animated about music. She could play a mean piano . . . but she couldn't sing.

Our parents adored Mrs. Teasdale. They even hosted a banquet in her honor to thank her for all she'd done for us. And they gave her an engraved plaque expressing their appreciation!

We, of course, were not invited to the banquet, which was just as well. We didn't see why our parents thought she was such an outstanding teacher.

Now, more than thirty years later, I understand why Mrs. Teasdale was so tenacious. We were inner-city, mostly-minority kids facing a multitude of challenges we couldn't anticipate at the tender ages of eleven and twelve. But our ferocious Bulldog knew the odds weren't in our favor, and she did everything she could to give us a leg up. She gave us the skills we needed to succeed in an occasionally hostile world. She made us believe we could achieve whatever we dreamed, and she gave us invaluable tools: sacrifice, discipline, fortitude, and responsibility. She wasn't a tyrant. She was exactly what we needed.

Tanya J. Tyler credits Mrs. Teasdale for the tenacity, determination, and discipline that helped her become a mother, a minister, and a writer. Her work has appeared in *Chicken Soup for the Single Parent's Soul, Chicken Soup for the Working Mom's Soul,* and *American Profile* and *Disciples World* magazines.

My Teacher, My Colleague, My Friend

Seema Bagai

The August afternoon sun glimmered. From my window, I had a perfect view of the green metal bench with a brass plaque attached to its center. The bench sat across the quad, at the edge of the grass, shaded by a mulberry tree and freshly planted roses. Soon, family, friends, and coworkers would gather for the dedication of the bench to celebrate the career of Wendy Livingston, my first-grade teacher, colleague, and friend.

Because I was so young, I don't remember specific events, but I do remember Mrs. Livingston's enthusiasm for teaching and that first grade was fun. We read, wrote, drew, sang, cooked, and painted. All these years later, I can close my eyes, picture the classroom, and almost see Mrs. Livingston moving about the room offering personal attention and praising each of us. Often, if I concentrate, I can recall the sound of her soft voice, but mostly I feel the love.

Mrs. Livingston inspired me to become an elementary school teacher, and—to my great delight—after teaching for several years in another district, I returned to teach fourth grade at my former elementary school. The minute I entered the office, she spotted me across the room. She looked older, of course, but time had not aged her smile or her gentle voice, which I recognized immediately.

"Remember me?" she called out, and I rushed over to hug her. After holding tight for several seconds, she leaned back to take a long look at me.

"Of course. You're Mrs. Livingston," I replied, amazed she recognized me after all these years. In my mind, she was still my first-grade teacher, not a colleague in the next classroom, so it was almost a year before I felt worthy of calling her simply Wendy.

Over the next several years, I would rely on Wendy's expertise and advice when faced with challenges. Wendy was now the school's resource-specialist teacher and worked almost exclusively with students who had learning disabilities. Her classroom door was always open, however, and she made time to offer ideas for working with students in my classroom. One year, one of my students needed additional help in reading. Wendy had learned about a new computer program that could assist this student, and without being asked, she obtained the computer and made the arrangements to have it equipped with the necessary software the student needed to receive the specialized lessons.

One year, when I learned the day before winter break that the carpet was going to be replaced in my classroom, I skipped the Christmas luncheon to put things away so they would be safe when the furniture was moved. Wendy found out about this and quietly slipped out of the party to bring me lunch. She then stayed to help pack my things.

At the next staff meeting, I wanted to thank Wendy for her help by giving her the staff star medal, awarded each month to a teacher for doing something special for another staff member. I had received the medal the previous month and eagerly selected Wendy to receive it next. I rehearsed what I wanted to say, mostly raves about her extreme thoughtfulness, when about two sentences in, Wendy rolled her eyes and waved her hand at me. She never wanted the spotlight on herself. To her, helping others was a natural act, not something deserving recognition.

One October evening, five years after I started teaching with Wendy, I received a phone call from a friend. Wendy had not been feeling well for weeks and had gone into the hospital for an operation. The friend called to tell me that they had discovered a malignant brain tumor. My heart plummeted and tears flooded my eyes. Over the next several months, I prayed every day for Wendy to recover, received updates through a mutual friend, and updated the staff on her progress. Each day, I expected to see Wendy walking across the quad or sitting in the staff room eating lunch just as she always did. For a time it appeared she would recover, but her prognosis abruptly became terminal.

On my final visit with Wendy, I took along a copy of my first-grade report card and a note she had written to my parents.

I wanted her to see that I had preserved those papers not only because they chronicled my history but largely because they were a reminder of our unique relationship.

Four months after her death, my father was diagnosed with the exact same illness. Having just experienced Wendy's nightmare, I understood what to expect. I already knew about the limited treatment options, about the rapid growth of this type of cancer, and that his life was about to come to an abrupt, heartbreaking end. Without ever imagining that it would become so essential, Wendy unknowingly taught me about cancer and dying. Her illness and her bravery throughout her final days had become her final lesson to me.

I took another long look out my classroom window at the memorial bench and then headed outside to greet Wendy's family who had just arrived for the event. After everyone left, I paused at the bench and ran my hands over the inscription on the plaque, which simply said, "In Loving Memory, Wendy Livingston, Devoted Teacher: 1977–2005." It's a solid, sturdy, beautiful bench and a marvelous tribute to Mrs. Livingston. She would love the idea of students sitting on the bench at lunchtime, enjoying the mulberry tree and roses. In time, all the students and most of the staff who knew her as well as I did will move on, but her bench will stand for a long, long time.

Seema Bagai is an elementary school teacher and writer. She lives in Southern California. In her free time, she enjoys reading and traveling.

Goodbye, Mr. P

Tammy Glaser

From the moment I squeezed into the desk chair, my stomach
was in knots. After two years attending a large junior-high in
an urban jungle, I was used to slipping under the radar and
remaining blissfully anonymous. Unfortunately, like all military families, we unexpectedly vacated one place for
another. I was delighted to escape the jungle, but
apprehensive about beginning my freshman year
in a tiny K–12 school in Newfoundland, Canada, where I was one of six freshmen and
painfully visible.

As if he noticed my reticence, Mr. Pilgrim,
Newfoundland's most sympathetic English
teacher, cheerily welcomed me and the only
other new student, Berta, to the class. "I can tell
that you two are going to be some of my prettiest girls ever," he said, his eyes dancing. "Not like

those dingbats!" He winked and pointed to the two giggling girls around our same age. Their giggles swelled, but I only worried briefly what they thought. Mr. Pilgrim had called me—a chubby teen with owlish glasses, unfashionable hand-me-down clothes, and a curly mop even Farrah Fawcett's hairdresser couldn't tame—pretty.

He extended our welcome by directing us to an ugly over-stuffed chair at the back of the classroom. "I always ask pretty girls to sign my chair, so get yourselves a pen, hustle on over there, and make your mark on the world." Berta and I headed over to what appeared to be a monument doodled upon by every student who had ever attended Mr. Pilgrim's class. Names and drawings covered the faded, sage-green fabric. We added our flourishes, and thus my freshman year began.

Mr. Pilgrim, whom we affectionately dubbed Mr. P, melted my fears with his easygoing attitude. His love for literature was apparent and infectious. Dressed casually in his polo shirt and slacks, he boyishly swept his bangs to the left just before sharing an exciting tidbit about an author. When he assigned books he was convinced we would love, his eyes literally twinkled, and he always found ways to bring the stories to life. Because Newfoundland's perpetually dreary weather could be unendurable, he assigned J. R. R. Tolkien's *The Hobbit* as the first book of the semester. Flashing his broad smile and puckish eyes, he described it as engaging adventure about mythical beings from an ancient age and suggested we burrow into its fantastical world. Late in the semester, on the one and only gorgeous day the Grand Banks would see that winter, Mr. P saw the sun peeking through the blinds and dropped the book he was holding. "Okay, everyone! Tell me everything you know about hobbits!" Satisfied with our descriptions, he escorted us outside, into the blaring sun, and off to the docks for an impromptu, "educational" field trip that he called "hobbit hunting."

I was still traumatized by my last school, where teachers seemed to assign gritty novels that reflected the grim surroundings. About the same time we were reading *Lord of the Flies*, a particularly mean-spirited boy had karate-kicked me in the face and broke my glasses. I began a daily dash from the classroom to my locker to avoid becoming the next Piggy. Images of lost kids angered by poverty, gangs, and drugs still haunted the hallways of my wounded psyche.

Mr. P's book recommendations soothed my soul, erasing memories of the urban jungle. Newfoundland, however, was so tranquil—and so isolated—we spent an inordinate amount of time indoors. Since we also only had two television stations and one radio station, our indoor activities were pretty much limited to hobbies, games, and books. On weekends, I cruised the base library, where I happily spent hours searching for authors Mr. P recommended.

However, not every book Mr. P assigned provided lightweight amusement. We tackled love and war in *The Iliad*, *Ivanhoe*, *Gone with the Wind*, and *For Whom the Bell Tolls*. And not every book fired my imagination: I didn't love *The Razor's Edge*, *Siddhartha*, or *Brave New World*. But I trusted Mr. P and plodded through heifers like *The Story of Mankind*, and galloped through others like *Goodbye, Mr. Chips*, simply because he said I should.

Like Mr. Chips, Mr. P's quips and stories won him undying affection. Unlike Mr. Chips, he was neither a strict disciplinarian nor steeped in tradition. What he had was a real gift for bringing his subjects to life. Even though we showed little interest in nineteenth-century art, he narrated a slide show of masterpieces by telling engaging stories about the artists that left us wanting more.

He also lured us into sports by making it fun. When a new, ambitious PE teacher wanted us to jog and most of us thought it was a bad idea, Mr. P was the only teacher to strap on sneakers and diligently work toward his "100-Mile Club" T-shirt. He joined us on most extracurricular activities, everything from basketball games and dances to fishing derbies and pie-eating contests. We spent a stormy, sleepless night camping at a bird sanctuary with an obnoxious foghorn. When a group of what he so affectionately termed "dingbats" (myself included) serenaded the teacher's tent with "Oh, What a Beautiful Morning" at daybreak, Mr. P was the only adult sporting a smile on his face.

For three years, I relished every moment spent in Mr. P's presence. Unfortunately, during my senior year, we received startling news. I was babysitting when the call came. My mother, her voice choking, delivered the news. "I have terrible news, honey . . . It's about Mr. P. He collapsed in his classroom after a run. I'm so sorry, darling, but he died."

"Died!" I set the phone down and literally wailed while my mother waited. "That's impossible! How could a vibrant man who jogged every day die so young? He's only thirty-five years old! He's fit and thin. He lifts weights with his sons in the weight room several times a week. It must be a mistake. Tell me it's a mistake, please, please!" But it wasn't a mistake. Speaking through tears, I broke the news to the girls in my care, and we left to join our fellow students. As the hours passed, student after student streamed into the small home where we gathered. We were inconsolable. Even the boys openly sobbed. None of us could imagine life without Mr. P and dreaded walking by his classroom in the coming weeks. So many parents called the principal concerned about their children's grief, he cancelled class on Friday, lengthening spring break by one day.

Mr. P was laid to rest in his favorite well-worn hunting clothes: washed-out overalls, beat-up boots, and a tacky fishing hat. The service was simple; the mourners were plentiful. Even though he was originally from Montana, Mrs. P knew that her husband would rather spend eternity in Newfoundland, close to his beloved students, so she had him buried near the base.

We all felt cheated that we never had a chance to say good-bye to our real-life Mr. Chips. In fact, we had only a single consolation during those dark days. When his heart clutched, our Mr. P sank into the ugly, overstuffed chair that hundreds of his loving students had signed. We liked to pretend he felt our final, collective hug and preferred to remember him dashing toward the door headed off to hunt hobbits in Elysian Fields.

Tammy Glaser, a 1985 graduate of the United States Naval Academy, lives in Manning, South Carolina, with her husband Steve. She has homeschooled her two children since 1995 and provides an e-mail list for families homeschooling children with autism on her blog available on *http://aut2bhomeincarolina.blogspot.com.*

A Tribute to Snow College

Sonja Herbert

When I left Germany with my American soldier husband in 1973 to live in the United States, we were weeks away from welcoming our first child. Since I had left school at age fourteen to work full time, I only had an eighth-grade education and barely spoke English; I depended upon my husband to make all the important decisions. I'd been in Utah about four years and had two children when he suggested that we join a religious community. I questioned its practice of polygamous marriages, but I relied on my husband's judgment. Hesitantly, yet full of religious zeal, I followed his lead.

When I was pregnant with my third child, in what I can only describe as a moment of divine intervention, I drove to the registrar's office at tiny Snow College in Ephraim, Utah, deposited $120 in cash to pay full tuition for one class, and humbly asked if I could please attend English 101. Convinced they would reject me due to my limited education, or because I belonged to a polygamous religion, I was surprised when the teachers welcomed me. When I earned an A in that first course, the college officials encouraged me to take English 102, and then English 103.

In 1981, pregnant with my fourth child, I put my haphazard education on hold. Two years later, when I was expecting my fifth child, my husband selected and married another woman, who became my "sister wife." Because she was not able to have children, she worked full time. "Why don't you take more college classes so you can get a degree," my husband said. "That way, you can get a good job later, and everybody will contribute to the family." So I returned to Snow College.

I cooked breakfast and dinner for everybody—every single day—studied after everyone went to bed, and often got up again at night with at least one of my children. Between the pregnancy and the demands on my time, I often debated the sanity of continuing to attend classes. One day, when feeling particularly tired, discouraged, and very pregnant, I waddled into history class. That day, the instructor, Roger Baker, tapped into an issue that ultimately changed my life, and he did it by simply writing a quote on the blackboard:

> *"Read not to contradict and confute, not to believe and take for granted, not to find talk and discourse, but to weigh and consider."—Sir Francis Bacon*

Mr. Baker gave the class a moment to read it, and then he asked what we thought Sir Francis Bacon meant when he wrote these words. When Mr. Baker ended the class that day, he said, "Not everything that gets printed is true. To get the most out of what you read, as Sir Francis Bacon said so eloquently, you need to 'weigh and consider it.' You have both the right, and the responsibility, to think about things, to find truth on your own." When he said this, he looked straight into my eyes, as if he knew the truth of my life and how much I needed to continue my education and work toward independence. To me, it was as if someone had turned on a light.

For days, weeks, and even months, I meditated on that quote and what it meant to my life. I finally realized that I, too, had the right to "weigh and consider" everything the church leaders wanted us to believe. They said everything they wanted us to believe came directly from God, but God had given me the ability to think—he must have wanted me to discover for myself whether or not other people's interpretations had validity or were simply their own version of the truth. I kept my rebellious thoughts to myself, but a fire was burning inside me. I became more determined than ever to continue my education.

My fifth child was born during semester break, and I returned to school when she was two months old. Even though I went to classes exhausted, Mr. Baker, who was teaching medieval history that semester, was, once again, a potent messenger. When he assigned subjects for our term papers, he seemed to purposefully choose Eleanor of Aquitaine for me.

With no idea what part she played in history, I soon learned she ascended to become a queen to both France and England without having been born into a royal house, and that she virtually single-handedly invented the Romantic movement. Eleanor also was brave enough to divorce the King of France so she could marry the young man who later became the King of England. When I compared my life to hers, I saw so many differences. I thought my husband loved me, but instead of doing great things for me, he seemed to humor me, as if I were a child. Studying Eleanor of Aquitaine made me see something in my marriage I had ignored for too long.

With five children, including an infant, attending classes became more and more challenging. Although one might have imagined him sensitive to disruption, my Spanish teacher Mr. Hendrikson allowed me to bring my squirming and squealing infant to class when I couldn't find a sitter. If we had a test that day, he would hold my baby in his arms and whisper Spanish endearments to her. Not only did it allow me to continue, it helped me understand that teachers were serving as my allies—that some teachers loved and accepted me enough to both honor and facilitate my desire for an education.

Although pregnant with my sixth child, I returned to Snow College the next year and studied Spanish, English grammar, and linguistics. When Mary Ann Christison, the linguistics instructor and head of the language department, asked me if I could find time to assist the teachers, I eagerly accepted. The work fit right into my schedule, and Mrs. Christison paid me enough to afford a babysitter.

When I finally earned an associate's degree, Mrs. Christison suggested that I apply for the state's Career Teaching Scholarship. "You have an excellent chance of winning," she enthusiastically explained. "The scholarship will pay all your tuition expenses and fees until you earn your Bachelor of Arts degree and teaching certificate." As if she could see the worry on my face, she leaned over and said, "And you will even receive a little extra to live on."

The day I received notice that I had, indeed, won the Career Teaching Scholarship, I bravely confessed to my husband that I was no longer willing to live in a polygamous marriage. Unsure of the steadiness of my resolve, let alone my legs, I asked him if he would consider leaving the religious community and surrendering my sister wife. Even though he was willing to consider leaving the group, he did not want to let go of his other wife. Ironically, he explained by saying, "She is not as resourceful as you, and she needs me much more than you do."

I rented a cheap apartment near the Southern Utah University in Cedar City and moved in with my six children. Over the course of the next two years, I earned a bachelor's degree in English, Spanish, and German, as well as a teaching certificate. Again, somewhat ironically, on the same day I completed my final tests—one year before graduation—my divorce, too, became final.

Since that day, I have taught high school, while also raising my six children to be educated and self-motivated human beings. I also eventually remarried, and returned to school, where I earned a master's degree in linguistics.

So my hero is not one teacher but the many teachers at Snow College who took their jobs very seriously. Because this small set of instructors took an interest in me, honored my quest for an education, guided me through a labyrinth of self-doubt and gullibility, and helped me find ways to overcome all my obstacles, I obtained the best education of all—a true education of the heart.

Sonja Herbert authored an award-winning biographical novel about her half-Jewish mother's survival of the Holocaust in a traveling circus, where Sonja was born. Excerpts from that novel, as well her essays, nonfiction, and fiction stories, have appeared in several anthologies, as well won honors and prizes. Learn more about her on *http://german-writer.com*.

The Proving Ground

Cynthia Rogan

During the summer of 1972, right before I started twelfth grade, I was ripped from my comfortable Florida life and transplanted to Chattahoochee Valley, Alabama, where my parents had grown up. The first day of school was brutal. In the hall between classes, I could feel the stares, hear the whispers of the other kids; a nagging reminder that I was not one of them. I walked alone, spoke only for the purpose of answering questions, and resigned myself to the belief that it was going to be a very long last year of high school.

I'd been assigned English with Mr. Hall—a man who had taught both my parents. He had probably taught everyone's parents. He'd been teaching since Methuselah wore training pants. As if to illustrate my nonchalance, I sat in his classroom, doodling smiley faces on the front of my binder while other students filed in, chatting about summer and catching up on gossip. I eavesdropped, looking up on occasion to observe the white-haired teacher my parents revered, although I couldn't fathom why.

Mr. Hall remained captivated by the paperback he was reading. *Probably Chaucer. Maybe Dickens.* I rolled my eyes, making no attempt to see the title of the book. I was convinced there was a factory that produced English teachers and felt this one would be disappointingly similar to the others I'd had throughout school—though definitely older.

When the bell rang, Mr. Hall put down his book and stood to face the class. After introducing himself, he surveyed the group in front of him, his manner as crisp as the white shirt he was wearing. He picked up a clipboard and began to call roll, pausing at each name to quiz the student about parent and sibling history, occasionally taking an anecdotal side trip.

When it was my turn, he peered into my eyes. "Miss Fetner," he said. "I believe you look like your lovely mother."

I blushed. "Thank you." That was it. He moved on, and I exhaled.

But secretly I liked the way he gave each student his due. He seemed to be searching for who we were beneath our teenage angst and bravado. I felt a calming rush of warmth and knew I would find my own place in that room, in Mr. Joe D. Hall's senior English class.

Very soon, despite the loathsome grammar reviews and my fear of public speaking, I looked forward to his class. Mr. Hall insisted we read aloud—sometimes an article from the *Valley Times News*, more often, some pearl from English literature.

If we had something to say, we were encouraged to address the class from his podium. At the first sign of apathy, Mr. Hall would introduce eclectic and thought-provoking topics to get us talking again—he loved ethics, moral dilemmas, and philosophical outlooks. On Monday, a typical debate may have involved a controversial penalty from a recent football game. Later that week, we would leave his classroom still arguing about the effect vandalism has on society.

Just before spring break, we discussed the subject of self-fulfilling prophecy. We had spent the entire class on Wednesday and Thursday tightening our grasp on the concept. If the theory was correct, looking for the best in people could make them act their best—toward me, toward everyone. Mr. Hall believed we could, and although I admired his faith in humanity, I wasn't convinced.

Friday, as students trickled into the classroom, Mr. Hall walked up and down the rows, placing an exam face down on each desktop. "Please take your seat and leave your papers as they are," he said, turning to scan the class. "Mr. Young?" he called to a student who had turned his test over for a head start.

"Here," the boy Young answered, not realizing he'd been caught. The class laughed. He grinned and put down his paper.

The teacher didn't lose his rhythm. "Miss Gearwood?" He returned to the names on the list until everyone had been accounted for. Then he leaned against his desk and, using his thumb and forefinger, attempted to tame his bushy white eyebrows. "Do all of you have something to write with?"

We gave a collective grunt and nod.

He picked up his satchel and walked to the open doorway. "There's a meeting in the office I must attend," he said, saluting the class. "I have faith that your integrity, and my trust in you will remain intact." He smiled and turned away. "You may begin."

Open-mouthed, I watched through the window as he walked down the long sidewalk toward the principal's office. *You've got to be kidding!* I'd always thought he was smarter than that. He had to know someone would cheat.

Before he disappeared around the corner, two class ruffians had already started asking for answers; the rest of us remained silent, our eyes glued to our own papers. Soon, they tried peeking over our shoulders, but—committed to earning the trust our teacher had already awarded us—we shielded our work from their view.

All these years later, I can't recollect the subject of the quiz, nor can I recall my score. What I remember is the remarkable teacher who restored my faith in humanity. He knew the vast majority of us would pass the *real* test . . . and that the cheaters would be a striking minority.

He allowed humanity to teach us an important lesson in the safety of his classroom—that most of us want to do the right thing.

Thank you, Mr. Hall.

***

Cynthia Rogan began writing poetry under the hall light as her parents and four siblings slept. During daylight hours she added short stories and essays. Many years later, after her three daughters had left home, she found the house far too quiet and decided it was time to start that novel. She is currently working on her second one.

On the Edge of My Seat

Judyann Ackerman Grant

Climbing high into the middle of an old apple tree, I cloaked my inner feelings of invisibility with an outer reality. Just as no one was aware of the inner pain I carried, I thought no one could see me hidden amid the leafy boughs. If I remained quiet on my perch, as siblings passed by, no one would hear me either. In the same vein, I felt no one heard my silent cries seeking help to escape an insecure childhood.

Nestled in my sanctuary, on the ancient tree's thick, gnarled limbs, I whiled away the hours, daydreaming of heroes who would come to my rescue. Most of my heroes were straight from books or television—they ranged from the kind and gentle Tin Man to the Lone Ranger. Other times heroes took the form of my latest childhood crush—Joey, the Elvis look-alike; Kenny, the fearless trouble-maker; or Lester, the tall quiet boy with deep-set eyes.

My favorite daydream, though, involved an armor-clad knight who would gallop up on his noble black steed. The hero was a dark-haired stranger, his face shrouded in masks and mystery. Yet I felt no fear as he swept me off my feet and carried me away to his kingdom of peace, happiness, and security.

The threads of my childhood were woven with fantasies. Since I was invisible, I was never "me." I didn't even know who "me" was. I coped with the difficulties of my life by imagining I was someone else—someone bold and courageous. Someone who wasn't afraid to leap into the unknown. But I remained, rooted, literally and figuratively, to my secret place in the apple tree, enduring a life of unfilled wishes.

While daydreams filled my days, they never made it onto paper—that is, until the day a teacher gave me a life-changing assignment.

It was the fall of 1967. Mrs. Engst, a shy, sweet woman, materialized as our freshman English substitute teacher. Due to the short notice and subsequent lack of curriculum plans, she assigned the class an off-the-cuff story to write. Permission to put my creative musings down on paper thrilled me. Mrs. Engst assigned class-time to begin our stories. Excitedly, I began scrawling a stream-of-consciousness Halloween mystery and filled two pages with dramatic scenes in which teenagers faced danger, forced bravado, and thwarted disaster. I handed in my assignment with a flourish.

When we came to class on Friday, Mrs. Engst said she had received many good stories and that she would read aloud the best one. "A story that had me on the edge of my seat," she said.

I looked around the room. Vicky, the super student, sat smugly, her hands clasped on the wooden desk as if she were ready to applaud her own efforts. Marty, the class clown, poked his neighbor, then puffed out his chest, sticking his thumbs through pretend suspenders.

Mrs. Engst introduced the story as "a scary Halloween tale about a teenage party in an empty house." She winked at me.

I fidgeted.

Vicky glared.

I blushed.

Marty looked over to see who Vicky was looking at.

And I squirmed.

Mrs. Engst was going to read *my* story! Me—a nobody! I felt dizzy and delirious with joy. Maybe now I wouldn't be invisible.

The room fell silent. A captive audience focused on Mrs. Engst. To me, what followed was pure heaven, the highlight of my high school career.

Two months after graduating, I was hired at a small-town weekly newspaper office to set type. Over the years I worked my way through every aspect of the business, from typing to advertising to design and darkroom work.

Stored in a back room of the newspaper office were stacks of brittle yellow newspapers, dating back to the mid-1800s. I spent lunch and coffee breaks reading old stories and articles and longed to share these hidden gems with others. That's when an old spark was rekindled. As if Mrs. Engst whispered it in my ear, I came up with an idea: a weekly column filled with historical tidbits gleaned from the pages of the newspapers.

My boss liked the idea, and "In the Beginning" debuted two weeks later. The column ran for several years and generated many complimentary letters to the editor.

A short time later I married my dark-haired stranger (who drove not a black steed but a green '64 Chevy Bel-Aire). Happy and content with my new life, I began keeping a journal. As the children arrived, I recorded their milestones. When our youngest headed to kindergarten, I took a leap of faith and contacted our church's denominational headquarters and asked if they needed a writer. They did.

Would I have become a writer if Mrs. Engst hadn't decided to read my story to the class that day? I'm not certain. As a child, I was convinced that I would never amount to anything. Yet, when Mrs. Engst encouraged me to capture a flight of fancy on paper, she unknowingly lit a spark in me. The pride I saw reflected in her eyes that day stayed with me and kept that spark flickering for years.

That shy, sweet substitute teacher is the one I credit with putting flesh on an invisible child. Her encouragement set the course for my life. Her positive words and praise laid a foundation of confidence in my heart. All these years later, I still vividly recall her unwavering enthusiasm. That memory calls me, time after time, to step out in a leap of faith—to step out on a limb.

Judyann Ackerman Grant has published numerous articles, devotions, meditations, and poetry for adults, and stories and Bible school curriculum for children. She has written an inspirational newspaper column for the past fifteen years and has authored three children's books.

Lesson from a Muse of Yore

Nancy Brewka Clark

She got off the bus at the bottom of the street, negotiating the metal steps with difficulty. She was old—no, ancient—and arthritis had nearly crippled her. Even so, she'd never missed a lesson yet, not even on a day like today when the air threatened to explode into torrents and thunder hung in the sky.

I watched as she began to limp up the incline, a heavy satchel banging against her flowered skirt. Her bowed legs were encased in heavy pink stockings, her feet entombed in heavy black orthopedic shoes. A black straw hat perched on her head, but I knew perfectly well what lay beneath: short wispy white hairs through which her scalp shone through pink as a baby's.

"Miss Lamb's almost here," I called to my sister, and the two of us ran giggling up our steep driveway. In the kitchen, we gobbled down chocolate chip cookies as we waited for the slow, inevitable knock on the front door. Our mother would answer it with the usual pleasantries before showing her into the room where our old upright piano waited, teeth bared for the slaughter.

Barbara and I were eleven and nine, respectively, and for as long as we could remember, we'd taken piano lessons from Miss Sylvia Lamb. Our father was a frustrated musician, a man with a wavering tenor and a complete inability to carry a tune. He loved music, however, and wished for his two daughters to be the stars he never could be. While his genes had given us the same tin ears and leaden fingers, he never seemed to hear our constant mistakes.

"Miss Lamb is really getting through to them," he'd say to our mother at the dinner table after our weekly lesson. Mum would just smile and pass the mashed potatoes, a far better critic than he at judging our talents. As much as she loved us, she knew that neither of us was bound to sit behind a shiny Steinway on *The Ed Sullivan Show*.

As for Miss Lamb, she was the perfect personification of her name, gentle, always patient, and meekly surrendering to the bitter blows of our little fingers upon the keys. And when she played a piece for us, demonstrating how it should sound, the notes frolicked like happy creatures gamboling in green fields, and her watery blue eyes would radiate pure joy. She loved music, and I could tell that she loved us just for listening.

"Now you try," she'd say in the quavering voice of the very old, breathing out the sweet scent of butterscotch. "Remember, play with your heart, and your hands will follow."

On this day of oppressive humidity and impending down-pours, a summer day when all of our friends were off at the beach or at camp or at least spitting water into each other's faces at the huge public pool, we polished off the last cookie without hearing the familiar knock. Sauntering into the living room and fanning ourselves ostentatiously with our hands, we found our mother standing at the screen door and staring down our sloping front lawn with its limp maples into the street.

"She's late," Mum said. "I hope nothing's happened to her."

Instantly my sense of relief vanished.

"Did you see her get off the bus?" our mother asked.

"Nancy did," Barbara said.

That sounded like tattling to me—but I hadn't done anything wrong!

"It looked like her," I mumbled. "All stooped and everything." I remembered how she'd been limping and added, "Maybe she fell."

Mum opened the screen door and stepped out onto the small porch with its two white pillars. After gazing up and down the silent street, she started down the shallow brick steps.

"There she is," Barbara called.

I looked in the direction she was pointing, and my heart jumped in my chest. Miss Lamb was sitting at the edge of the sidewalk just across the street, fanning herself with her hat. Her satchel had sprung open, shifting various melodies out onto the concrete.

"Stay there," Mum called. She ran down the rest of the lawn and across the broiling black tar where she bent over Miss

Lamb, talking to her so softly we couldn't hear a thing. Then she turned. "Get Miss Lamb a glass of water. And bring a cold facecloth."

Barbara and I ran into the house. Not bothering to let the water run cold, we shoved a glass under the tap. When it was full, I turned and ran with it, slopping some of it onto the linoleum. Barbara ran behind me screaming, "Don't drop it, clumsy." Neither of us remembered to bring the damp facecloth.

By the time we made it across the street, Mum had scooped up the spilled music and put it back in the satchel. Miss Lamb had put her hat back on her head. Our piano teacher's wrinkled face was yellow beneath the old-fashioned powder she wore on her face, her eyes strangely vague.

When I handed her the water, Miss Lamb fixed me with a strange grin, revealing ill-fitting dentures as yellow as her complexion. "Now you try," she said.

"Miss Lamb, don't you want to get up?" I asked, offering her both hands.

She looked at them. "You can tell from the fingers." She gave me the same strange grin. "Now you try."

Ordering us to stay with Miss Lamb, Mum hurried next door, where Mrs. Mackenzie had the almost unheard-of luxury of a second car. Fortunately, she was at home, and soon the two of them were heading toward the three of us now sitting on the curb. Barbara and I had decided to flank her in case she tried to get up and run away, but Miss Lamb stayed put, uttering only one sentence in the quaint idiom of her Maine youth: "Hot, ain't it?"

Giving us another order to go inside and stay there until she returned, Mum and our neighbor got Miss Lamb into the front passenger seat and took off for the hospital.

Barbara and I did as we were told. Listening to the thunder rumbling closer, we sought shelter in Daddy's den, where the upright piano sat like the ghost of a brown bear.

"I hope she comes back," I said. "I love the piano." I added after another moment, thinking of that heavy satchel and those high bus steps, "I love Miss Lamb."

Tired of playing second fiddle, Barbara merely sniffed. "You would."

Although she'd suffered nothing more serious than a slight heatstroke, Miss Lamb decided that she'd had enough of slippery fingers and long bus rides. My sister Barbara decided that she'd had enough of the piano. That autumn, Daddy found me another teacher. It was hate at first sight and it was mutual. He was all business, technical and cold, and when I played for him he scrunched his face up into a mask of massive disapproval and said I'd learned nothing, nothing at all.

But I had.

Nancy Brewka Clark is a lifelong devotee of Nathaniel Hawthorne, thanks to her piano teacher, Miss Sylvia Lamb, who gave her a complete set of his works. A member of Sisters in Crime, Nancy enjoys writing in different genres, including nonfiction for Adams Media's *Cup of Comfort* and *Rocking Chair Reader* series, and many short-short plays and monologues produced here and abroad. Her most recent poetry appears in *Visiting Frost*, published by The University of Iowa Press and *The North American Review*.

Eating the Elephant

Vaughn C. Hardacker

In October 1975, I was dreading a long, dark, and dreary northern Maine winter on unemployment. Once a proud marine, after two tours of duty, including service in Vietnam, I was lucky if I landed dead-end jobs, mostly as a construction laborer. I was married with a small child, and I only had two prospects for my long-range future: grim and none.

Finally, days before yet another lay-off, the Veterans Administration notified me that they had reviewed my case and assessed me 100 percent disabled for service-connected pulmonary tuberculosis. It should have been a huge relief, but it presented yet another dilemma. I could finally invest money and time in learning a trade, but I had no idea what to pursue.

Like most unmotivated teens from blue-collar families in the 1960s, I had been an average student in high school—except for math, where I was so far below average earning a D seemed like a major accomplishment. If you couldn't pass math, you couldn't go to college, so I joined the Marines. Unfortunately, being in the marines had done nothing to bolster my math scores. I was, however, a married man with a child, and I needed a plan.

Since college was out, I spent hours in the library systematically researching "how one (with limited opportunities) should determine what he wanted to do with his life." To a hardened Marine, most of it appeared to be a crock, but I discovered one common denominator that gave me a rather feeble clue: Find something that you liked and that would hold your interest. Okay, this part wasn't difficult. I quickly narrowed it down to three things: reading, watching television, and playing sports. I didn't know of any jobs that paid someone to read novels all day, so that was out. As for playing sports, I was in my late twenties, and while I could hold my own in the bush league that was the booming metropolis of Caribou, Maine, I was never going to be a professional baseball player. That left television. Why not? I could go to school to learn how to repair radios and televisions! However, one huge obstacle stood in the way: Televisions and radios are electronic devices, and learning electronics required an aptitude for math.

I sat up all night stewing over my problem. Up to that point, only a select few members of my family had finished high school, and none had gone to college. There was a point in high school when I fantasized about becoming a veterinarian, but I could not find a single curriculum that did not include at least one math course. Then, as now, given my history with math, I was convinced going to college would result in failure. Fortunately, my time in the military had taught me that if you made up your mind to do something, set a goal, and gave it your best, you could do it. Before I ruled electronics repair out, I decided to talk to someone at the Northern Maine Vocational Technical Institute. It couldn't hurt, and all it would cost would be a few hours of my time.

I spent about twenty minutes glossing over my qualifications—or rather my lack of qualifications—with the admissions director, who reminded me of a used-car salesman and whose name I no longer remember. He didn't care about whether or not I could complete the course. His only interest was in enrolling me to meet his quota. He ushered me across campus to the electronics lab and introduced me to Gordon Burgess, the head of the electronics department and the man who would ultimately save me. While the admissions director exhibited the false optimism of most high-pressure sales people, Gordon seemed nonchalant. Yet there was a glint in his eye that told me there was more to this man with the friendly, laid-back exterior. Feeling desperate to find a path, once the admissions director had sauntered back to his office, I decided to reveal my math phobia to Gordon.

Gordon grinned. "How do you eat an elephant?"

After I stood there for several seconds, probably with my mouth open, trying to come up with the answer to the stupidest question I'd ever heard, he said, "One bite at a time. That's how, and you, my friend, are going to learn college-level math—one bite at a time." He went on to explain his logic. "If you look at the whole elephant, the task would seem out of your grasp. But if you take one tiny, manageable bite, chew it for a long time, digest it, and then go back for another bite, and then another, over the course of many months, you will have eaten the entire elephant."

I plunked down the dregs remaining in my budget and enrolled in the class.

During the next two years, Gordon carved up the math elephant, and I ate those bites—one by one. I graduated from that course at the top of my class and—realizing college was, ultimately, just another elephant—enrolled in the University of Maine, where I earned my bachelor's degree in business management, and where I also went on to obtain a master's degree in business administration.

Over the years, I lost touch with Gordon, but I have never forgotten the kindness in his face, the magic in his logic, or his patience and dedication to the art of teaching. Armed with my fancy degrees, I proudly carried on his legacy. I spent ten years teaching electronics to underprivileged students who barely graduated from Boston and Chicago's inner-city schools. I always made it a point to meet with applicants who expressed concerns about passing math. I wasn't as smooth as Gordon. I always had to fight to keep from smiling at the expression on their faces when I coolly asked, "How do you eat an elephant?"

Vaughn C. Hardacker carried on Gordon's legacy as a high-technology trainer for over twenty years. He is also a published author, whose work has appeared in several periodicals. His novel, *The War Within*, was a runner-up in a major literary contest, and he is currently working on a mystery/suspense novel. He lives in New Hampshire.

A Teacher for Life

Arline Chandler

Born in 1918 to a hardworking farm couple, my Aunt Zula grew up in a three-room house built from rough boards and wood shingles and heated by a stone fireplace. After her mother became ill, Aunt Zula took on many household tasks, standing on a bench to reach the washtub and scrub clothes on a rub board when she was only eight. Despite a lack of funds and the commonly held belief that women didn't really need an education, Aunt Zula's thirst for knowledge could not be quelled. She attended school every day until she graduated from Wilburn High School in 1937, the first class in that tiny Arkansas school to have traditional graduation exercises.

Following graduation, she worked with the National Youth Association, one of President Roosevelt's New Deal projects. Through that organization, she enrolled at Arkansas State College (now Arkansas State University) in Jonesboro. To pay her expenses, Aunt Zula worked in the school's cafeteria; to buy a needed pair of shoes, she cleaned house for a professor.

Back in 1940, a sixty-hour certificate qualified a teacher for the classroom. As soon as she acquired one, Aunt Zula accepted a teaching position in a one-room school. Heat came from a wood stove; drinking water came from a spring. For her services, she received $40 a month, with a quarter of that amount allotted for room and board in a family's home. "I shared my bedroom with the grandma who lived with them," Aunt Zula often remembered, "and I walked the four miles home every weekend."

In the meantime, she fell in love with Reedy Turney, the redheaded agriculture teacher in the Quitman school district. Since Aunt Zula's teaching position ended in the spring, when youngsters had to help plant crops, the couple set a wedding date on an early April afternoon in 1941. The newlyweds packed Aunt Zula's meager clothing and a few linens into her husband's new Chevrolet truck and drove twenty-five miles from Wilburn to Quitman, Arkansas, where they began a life anchored by school and church and family. "Women typically did not work after marriage, so I gave no thought to a teaching career," Aunt Zula explained.

A baby daughter arrived in 1942, and three more children followed. "During those years of tending babies while doing laundry on a wringer washing machine and producing a large vegetable garden, I decided that diapers, bottles, and sleepless nights would be my life's work," Aunt Zula said.

Time marched on. Her toddlers grew to school age, but the endless mound of laundry, daily meals, sewing, and gardening still dominated Aunt Zula's life. And then, one fateful day, the Quitman school superintendent came to call. He needed someone to fill out the year for a fifth-grade teacher. He urged Aunt Zula to enroll in a college correspondence course and then pick up additional hours during the summer to complete her degree, which could lead to a permanent teaching position.

"I turned him down," she said, laughing. "Why, I had a family of six, a cow to milk, and a garden to tend. However, my husband thought I could do anything and thought it was a good idea, so I took it on."

During her first terms, she took correspondence courses and attended Saturday classes, as well as summer school, which required daily forty-mile drives to and from school. "I gathered vegetables from the garden, and had everything ready for my oldest daughter to prepare lunch the next day. After class, I put on the pressure cooker and studied while vegetables processed for canning."

Her husband's resolve proved fortunate when he was stricken with a brain tumor while their oldest daughter attended college and the other three children still lived at home. "After their dad's death, I didn't know if I could raise two teenage sons on my own," Aunt Zula lamented. "I felt so alone, but I managed on my teacher's salary to send all four of my children to college. We had some bumps, but they grew into responsible, productive adults."

In a town of less than 800 people, most of Quitman's permanent residents passed through Aunt Zula's classroom. In restaurants or shops in the tiny town, adults greet her with a hug, recalling that she was their teacher. "My students have become doctors, lawyers, merchants, truck drivers, waitresses, mothers, nurses, and teachers," Aunt Zula said, bursting with pride. "And to my regret, a few have ended up in jail."

At age eighty-nine, her once-lithe body stoops, her hearing is slight, and she walks with a cane; yet she continues to mentor other teachers in her hometown school and cluck-hen a passel of grandchildren around her knees. Her oldest grandson started bringing kids home from Harding University, saying that he merely had to say he was going to Grandma's house, and soon twenty friends lined up. Other grandsons and granddaughters followed suit. Aunt Zula puts mattresses on the floor and makes couches into beds. Her table groans with abundant food, and meals come to life when she shares her many stories, impressing her latest "students" with her charm and fortitude.

The character and knowledge she molded into young lives— her own children and grandchildren, her nieces and nephews, and those growing up in Quitman, Arkansas, who were lucky enough to be her students—are invaluable.

Arline Chandler credits her beloved Aunt Zula with setting the standard for her own motherhood and career as a kindergarten teacher. Chandler's work has appeared in *Workamper News, Ozarks Magazine, Coast to Coast, Motorhome,* and *Branson's Review.* She has also authored three books and teaches classes at the Ozark Folk Center, Mountain View, Arkansas. View excerpts of her work on *www.arlinechandler .com.*

My Mother, My Teacher

Samantha Ducloux Waltz

I frowned at the page, crossed out a word, and scribbled in another. "I'm not happy with this story," I said, linking eyes with the members of my weekly writing group. "Something's missing, but I'm not sure what."

Tim nodded in agreement. "It's well written. It's clever. But it isn't quite . . . I don't know . . . it doesn't quite have . . ." He shook his head.

I tapped my pen against the manuscript and chewed my lip. "My mother would know what it needs," I said, and then laughed nervously.

Everyone except Tim rustled their papers and fidgeted in their seats. Tim, who had recently come on board, had been spared multiple essays about my troubled relationship with my mother. "She *would* know," I explained. "For all her faults, she *was* the best teacher I ever had."

Because writing groups are often as much about probing writer's block as they are about the work, I launched into a story. "Let me give you a picture. I'm seven years old, sitting on a little stool beside her typing table, carefully printing stories on a pad of wide-lined paper while she taps out her novels, nonfiction books, and essays on her Underwood. "How do you spell 'bridle'?" I ask. I'm writing my first novel about how a boy saves a colt injured at birth and they become best friends.

"Mother looks up from her typewriter. "B-r-i-d-l-e," she says. "The boy must be starting to train the colt. Be sure to give the reader a lot of detail. You might want to find a book in the library about training horses."

"So your mother was a writing teacher? That must have been interesting," Tim interjected.

"She taught "Writing for Publication" at the local college and sponsored annual writing conferences, as well as writing books and essays. While most mothers in her day would sweetly ask if you'd like a cookie, my mother would sweetly ask if my story had solid plot structure and reflected character development. She was incredibly and indelibly focused. It was like living in a permanent writing residency."

I put down my pen and reached for a cookie, took a teensy bite, and then continued. "My mother *was* a phenomenal teacher. When she lectured at local high schools, she'd have the rowdiest boys paying rapt attention within seconds. Some of her writing students became very successful authors. And they only had her for a class once a week. I had the opportunity to learn from her every day."

"So what happened to that first novel?" Tim asks.

"I grew discouraged with it, of course. So she showed me the children's page of a church magazine with drawings and stories by children my age and blithely asked, 'Would you like to do something like this?' Of course I did, so once I had an idea, she led me through the process of drafting, revising, and submitting my story. It was published, and my dream of becoming a writer was launched."

While everyone took another look at the pages I'd brought to critique, I took a second bite of cookie and thought again of my mother. She *was* a great teacher. But somewhere along the line I got tired of being her star pupil. I wrote avidly right through my teen years—keeping a diary that I locked each night and slid into my top drawer; contributing a story to the *Pasadena Star News* children's page; or writing an essay for a citizenship contest. *American Girl* magazine even published my winning essays.

Mother and I discussed each and every one of my writing projects, from research papers for school to reports for honor badges for Girl Scouts. I occasionally attended her evening classes, and I often attended her writing conferences. After all, the neatly dressed woman at the podium was an extraordinary teacher, and I thirsted for knowledge. I was proud of her and often wished my teachers at school came up with equally fascinating stories to illustrate each of their points.

But more and more I wanted her to sometimes drive a carpool, or have a neighbor over for a cup of coffee. I wanted to talk with her about how bad I felt when I wasn't invited to a friend's birthday party, or how I wanted a cute boy in my science class to ask me to the after-school dance.

Later, when I became a teacher and was raising three children, our writing liaison continued. Every time I crafted a parenting book, a juvenile novel, or an article, I'd send Mother a draft and she'd send it back within a week with comments scribbled around the edges of every page. She came to help with my babies. and would knit them sweaters and booties and caps. When I worked up the courage to leave my husband, my mother/teacher/mentor lent me the down payment for a house; but every conversation with her quickly led back to her omnipresent question, "What writing project are you working on now?"

"Writing was all we could ever talk about for more than three minutes," I said, returning my attention to the group.

"Well, it sounds to me like talking about writing was her way of connecting with you," Tim offered.

We did share a passion for writing. We both wrote stories to celebrate our joy and to grieve something or someone we'd lost. It's how we made sense out of a world that could be exciting and rewarding, or crazy and cruel. And talking together about our work was the way we shared our thoughts and feelings. I sighed deeply. "Still, I would have liked her to say, as a mother, that she loved me."

Tim looked surprised. "She obviously loved you! She dropped everything for you even when she was focused on her own writing."

The other group members raised their eyebrows and nodded silently in agreement.

I laughed at the irony! "You're right, of course you're right. Teaching me was her act of selfless love. She obeyed the cardinal rule of writing—show, not tell. Now that you mention it, when writing, she refused to take phone calls, entertain friends, or schedule appointments, but she allowed me to interrupt her 10,000 times when I lived at home. And when I moved away, she set everything else aside to talk about an idea on the phone or edit a manuscript I'd sent by mail. My mother showed me great love by teaching me to write—and by sharing her precious gift for teaching with the child she loved. Now that's a mother . . . and a teacher!"

Samantha Ducloux Waltz's essays can currently be seen in the *Cup of Comfort* Series, *Chicken Soup for the Soul* series, and a number of other anthologies. She has also published adult nonfiction and juvenile fiction under the names Samantha Ducloux and Samellyn Wood. She lives in Portland, Oregon.

A Lasting Impression

Mitzi L. Boles

After what seemed like a hundred stops and starts along bumpy rural roads, the school bus finally arrived, brakes squealing, at its destination. I drew in a deep breath and navigated the steps while clutching my book bag in one hand and my stuffed kitty tight against my chest.

When I opened the door to my first-grade classroom, all eyes magnetically gravitated in my direction. I could feel my cheeks turning a deep shade of pink.

"Good morning! Miss Boles, is it?" The teacher smiled warmly. "I'm Mrs. Gerard. We're just getting started. You can have a seat over there," she pointed toward an empty desk in the middle row.

I liked how she called me Miss Boles, and I felt relieved when she didn't ask why I was late and didn't make me sit in the front row. Her wavy hair was sprinkled with gray, and she wore small, spherical glasses. Her face looked relaxed, kind, and reassuring, and she seemed soft and huggable, like she was somebody's favorite aunt.

When the recess bell rang, not wanting to get caught in the crush, I lingered behind.

"Nice hair!" A burley boy with freckles tapped me on the head as he ran past me.

I shrunk back and blushed. My parents had argued about not being able to afford a haircut for my first day of school, so I decided to do it myself. I took my mother's scissors from her sewing table and chopped off several inches. It looked crooked so I chopped more, and then more. The end result was bone-straight hair in a ragged bowl shape with spiked bangs.

"It's not so bad," whispered a voice behind me. I turned around and looked square into Mrs. Gerard's eyes. They looked soft, trusting, and mildly amused. "Sometimes new ideas become popular when somebody is brave enough to try something different."

I knew she was just saying that to help me feel better, but within a few days I liked going to school, sitting in Mrs. Gerard's class, basking in the feeling that she liked me. One morning, after hopping off the bus, a mean older boy blocked my path.

"Let me see your little bitty kitty, baby," he demanded.

I held Janie as tightly as I could, but he ripped her out of my arms so abruptly her head fell to the ground and cotton fluff burst from her neck onto the cold pavement. I screamed in anguish.

"Tough break, kid," said the bully, and then nonchalantly tossed my kitty's body to the ground.

I scooped Janie up, shoved her body and her head into my book bag, and ran to my classroom, fighting tears. No one seemed to notice as I sank into my chair.

I was still so rattled and hurt when the recess bell rang, I jumped. Although everyone hurried outside, I couldn't move. I was suddenly paralyzed, unable to even lift my head, which I had laid on top of the desk. I was afraid to go outside, afraid someone else would tease me or do something to hurt me. Her skirt made a swishing sound as Mrs. Gerard slid into the seat next to me and gently cleared her throat.

"You were very quiet in class this morning. Is there something you would like to talk about?" Her sympathetic manner convinced me that it was safe to tell her so I pointed to my book bag. When she removed the pieces of Janie from the bag, my eyes brimmed with tears and my lips quivered, so she reached over and she put her hand on mine, and we sat quietly for several minutes. Finally, Mrs. Gerard asked softly, "Who did this?"

"The bully who sits at the back of the bus. I don't know his name."

"I see," she responded, sighing. When I looked into her deep blue eyes, she smiled. "Mitzi, would you let me take Janie home with me tonight?"

"Okay," I muttered. "My mom didn't want me to bring Janie to school anyway, so she'll be mad when she sees what happened."

"You might be surprised at how understanding she'll be if you just tell her the truth. It wasn't your fault."

The next morning Mrs. Gerard pulled Janie out of a bag and showed me where she had carefully stitched Janie's head back where it belonged! "She was very brave," Mrs. Gerard said, "and the scar isn't so bad, is it?" She had tied a beautiful pink bow around her neck to hide the jagged threads that held her neck in place.

"You fixed her! You fixed her! Thank you."

"You're welcome, Miss Boles. I was happy to help, but perhaps Janie would be happier staying at home from now on."

I nodded my head and smiled one of my biggest smiles.

Because I loved her, I was eager to do well in Mrs. Gerard's class and learn as much as I could, but I struggled with mathematics. When I got one of my papers back full of red marks, I felt so disappointed and embarrassed, I hung my head down. Mrs. Gerard asked me to bring my paper up and talk to her after class.

When everyone left, I trudged up the aisle to her desk. "I think we have a little problem here," she said, tapping the paper I had laid on her desk. The worksheet asked us to circle the larger of two numbers.

"I didn't have a ruler."

"A ruler?" Mrs. Gerard responded with surprise.

"The two really did look bigger than the seven."

"I see," said Mrs. Gerard, smiling. She put her fingers to her lips, the way grownups did when they knew they shouldn't laugh, when they were supposed to be serious. "Mitzi, what do you like?"

I dragged my fingers across her desk, stalling. "Ummm . . . horses, drawing, and stuff." And then I told her in a rush that the newspaper was having a drawing contest. "My mom read about it and told me I should send in a picture, but I don't think I can do it."

"Why not?" she asked.

"I really want to win, but I'm not very good. I'm only six."

"What do you have to draw?"

"They want a picture about the man who discovered America."

"Columbus?"

"Yeah, that's the guy!" Mrs. Gerard knew everything.

"You know, I think there is only one thing worse than not winning."

"What's that?" I asked, dipping my head slightly, paying close attention.

"Not trying at all," she said, pausing to capture my eyes.

Even to a first grader that really made sense.

A few days later, Mrs. Gerard held a newspaper up so that everyone could see. "Look, everyone," she crowed, "The newspaper had a drawing contest, and Mitzi Boles won!" After everyone clapped, she laid the paper on her desk and invited my classmates to gather around to admire the picture. It was only a stick-figure man arriving on land by boat, but some kids told me they thought it was very good, and I was thrilled.

Mrs. Gerard made a lasting impression. Because of her, I recognize how the smallest gestures can inspire a child in a very significant way. A heroic teacher isn't necessarily one who earned fancy degrees or became a brilliant college professor who publishes articles and wins awards. A heroic teacher often comes in the form of a first-grade teacher who merely pays close attention to what her students need and finds little ways to show them concern, and love, and faith. A heroic teacher teaches compassion, trust, belief, kindness, and host of other important life lessons through being a living example. Sometimes it's as simple as sewing the head back on a stuffed kitty.

Mitzi L. Boles is a freelance writer living in Payson, Arizona, with her husband and daughter. For nearly twenty years she worked in the field of education, at levels ranging from preschool assistant to community college instructor. She shares her passion for writing with wildlife rescue, and is currently working on a series of wildlife conservation books for children.

Pound for Pound

Paula Munier

Pound for pound: a boxing expression—the superior fighter, as judged by skill rather than weight.

Over the past five decades, I've had more teachers than I can count. They've come from every walk of life—educators, musicians, dancers, artists, Girl Scout leaders, clergy, editors, publishers, CEOs, realtors, lawyers, and the perennial IT professional. But I didn't meet the teacher from whom I would learn the most until I was forty-nine years old.

I was facing fifty in the face—and I was not ready. Still nursing my wounds after the end of an abusive relationship, I felt weak, physically, emotionally, and spiritually. I wanted to feel strong in every way as I hit the big five-oh. I figured I'd start with my body, so I signed up for the sport that in my mind most represented strength. *Boxing, the sweet science.*

The South Shore Boxing Club sprawls over the second floor of an old brick warehouse across from the train station in Whitman, Massachusetts. The first floor is devoted to paintball; most people park up front by the paintball entrance. To get to the gym, I have to drive to the end of the lot, where the lighting is poor and a big sign on a tall fence reads *Danger: Electrical Hazard.* It's the sort of place where a woman wouldn't want to find herself alone for very long. Unless, of course, she knows how to throw a punch.

Inside it's not much less intimidating. This is no ladies fitness center, where women in color-coordinated workout clothes do aerobics and practice Pilates moves in front of wall-to-wall mirrors. This is a huge open space. One side is filled with two regulation-size rings, the other sports an assortment of heavy bags and speed bags. A row of deep shelving houses gloves and mitts and jump ropes. The ceilings are high; the long windows are dingy; the worn brick walls are covered with posters. *Muhammad Ali. Jersey Joe Walcott. And the South Shore's own Rocky Marciano.*

Joey Robles is only five-foot-five, some three inches shorter than I. He's young and handsome and carries himself with the easy assurance of a tough kid from Brockton. But at 145 pounds of hard muscle, with tattoos decorating his bulging biceps and fierce forearms, Joey nonetheless looks the part he has played in my life since that fateful evening some two years ago: boxing coach. His own boxing career sidelined when he nearly lost an eye in an accident at his day job, Joey turned to training fighters.

"It's pugilism," Joey tells me by way of introduction. "Not boxing."

"Pugilism," I repeat solemnly.

He grins at me. "So when you write about it, you get it right."

Joey knows I am a writer. I have come here under cover; being a writer allows me to do things I'd never have the courage to pursue if I had to rely on purer motives. I've told Joey I'm here because I'm writing a novel in which my heroine must fight her way out of a few tight spots, and I want to get it right. This is partly true, but the larger truth is that I'm here for myself.

Joey shows me how to wrap my hands, then hands me a jump rope. He turns on the timer, and explains how it works. "We do everything in three-minute rounds. We work for three minutes, then we rest for one minute."

"Okay." I jump for a couple of rounds and think I am going to die.

I gulp for air while Joey slips my hands into my gloves. The next forty-five minutes is a blur of jabs, crosses, hooks, and upper cuts; feinting and footwork; heavy bag and speed bag. Just when I think it can get no worse, Joey pulls off my gloves and points to the padded floor of the ring. "Push-ups and sit-ups and you're done."

I am beyond weary, slick with sweat, trembling with muscle fatigue. But I drop down to my knees anyway.

"You can do it," Joey assures me, as he cheerfully pushes me through six sets of hell.

And to my everlasting surprise, I can.

By the end of my first lesson, I am exhausted—and euphoric. *Endorphin rush,* I'm thinking, as I roll my hand wraps back up and toss them into my bag. Joey watches me with far more interest than such rolling usually inspires.

"There are three kinds of people who come here," Joey says. "People who want to hurt other people. People who've been hurt by other people. And people who love the sport." He pauses, and looks at me.

I avoid his glance, intent on my rolling. I guess my writer cover hasn't fooled him. "I would be number two," I mumble, more to myself than to Joey.

He nods. "People who want to hurt other people we throw in the ring and teach a lesson. They never come back. People who love the sport we train to fight professionally."

Joey pauses again. "People who've been hurt we teach to fight so they can defend themselves the next time. And we teach them that it's okay to hate someone once in a while. We're going work out that anger with the gloves."

This time I raise my head and smile at him. "That sounds good."

"The confidence you gain will change your life," Joey tells me. "And I'm not just talking about pugilism."

Two years and counting, I am stronger than I have ever been in my life. My biceps and triceps rival those of most men my age; my forearms are rock hard. I walk taller, buoyed along by a torso tightened by constant twisting and legs honed by rounds and rounds on my feet. This physical assurance is one I've never before known—and one that carries over into the rest of my life. I am less accommodating, more assertive, feistier and tougher in every way. Knowing I can take care of myself physically has given me the same confidence to take care of myself in other ways as well.

Don't get me wrong. I'm still no Laila Ali—and never will be. But even though I may always be a palooka in the ring, thanks to Joey, today I am pound for pound the bravest I have ever been.

Because pound for pound, there's no teacher like Joey.

Paula Munier is director of innovation for Adams Media. She is also president of the New England Chapter of Mystery Writers of America. Her stories and essays have appeared in numerous anthologies, and she's a diehard boxing enthusiast. She lives in Pembroke, Massachusetts, with her son Mikey, two dogs, and a cat.

Mrs. Annibale—Aunt Lenora, to Me

Aimee Cirucci

I've always been drawn to teachers. Maybe even oddly attached to them. Both of my parents are teachers; they met in the classroom, a teacher and a student teacher assigned to work together. In high school, though I struggled finding friends my own age, I never struggled finding friends in teachers. I often spent lunchtimes chatting with Mrs. Wagner (Spanish), Mr. Edmonson (history), and Mr. Regan (chemistry). In retrospect, I seem the quintessential kiss-up, but these friendships were not motivated by a need to please. They began and endured because I found teachers to be smart and generous and interesting.

It would be easy to call any one of these teachers a mentor. But there is only one who stands out. Not a college teacher, not a Ph.D., not a junior high instructor who piqued my interest in history, not an elementary school teacher who turned me on to books, but my preschool teacher. She is the one who made the biggest difference.

Mrs. Annibale—Aunt Lenora, to me—was one of my first teachers and definitely the first teacher I remember. She taught me not just how to learn but how to live. Aunt Lenora taught preschool at First Baptist Church with her trademark zest for life. She wore clothing more appropriate for a day in New York City than a classroom of three- and four-year-olds—but that was the point. To her, being with us was more important and exciting than a day in the city and thus worthy of celebration. And we knew it.

Those of us in the class quickly became used to her demonstrative and unconditional love. In an era when teachers were encouraged to maintain space between themselves and their students, she was a rebel. She affectionately called us her "pigeons" and routinely showered us with hugs and compliments. She created an environment of affirmation and self-esteem before they became buzzwords. And it wasn't something she picked up in a book or at a workshop; it was the way she lived life, choosing to find and focus on the positive in everyone. Even when hyperactive and stubborn, we were praised for our activity, convictions, and the heights of our jumps. Scraped knees and setbacks were handled with Band-Aids, backrubs, and encouragement. More than twenty-five years later, a former preschool student spotted Aunt Lenora dining out and rushed over to share that being called a "pigeon" was her most enduring school memory. That story alone is proof that it's not what people do or say but how they make us feel that is important. And we felt loved.

Aunt Lenora made and continues to make ordinary occurrences extraordinary. Breakfasts at her home involved fluffy Belgian waffles that we ate off delicate china, outside, in our pajamas; trips to visit my cousin at college included wild car games, Italian cookies, and her trademark sports obsession. Soon, we were all living for every Penn State punt, as we listened along with her to the radio. She told great stories because she lived them, whether shooing an errant squirrel out of her house or blaming a missing jelly doughnut on the dog.

Life isn't always grand, of course, but the lesson Aunt Lenora teaches is that finding and fueling the grand and, above all, believing makes life worth living. "The Secret" was never a secret to her. Untrained as a teacher, with only a high school education, she rose to become one of the most popular preschool teachers at her school, eventually landing a job teaching kindergarten in one of the toniest areas in the state. Parents probably assumed she had degrees in childhood education and certifications in teaching; in truth, she had something more potent—wisdom in living.

That wisdom was tested in the fall of 1999. Lenora and her mother were closer than best friends, so it was unbelievably difficult when my grandmother was diagnosed with terminal lung cancer. My aunt immediately left work to care for her. I was away at college and absent for the most heart-wrenching days and months that led up to her death around Thanksgiving.

I can't fathom the loss of a best friend and mother in such a slow and painful fashion. My aunt lived it and emerged phoenix-like with her trademark humor, grace, and passion for life intact.

Six months after my grandmother's death, I graduated from college.

Shortly after returning home, I got a call from Aunt Lenora one afternoon, "Are you at home?"

"Yes," I said. "Why?"

"I am coming by to get you."

"What are we doing; where are we going?" I asked.

"Don't worry about it. I am picking you up, just trust me," she said.

And I did.

I got in the car as instructed, and she drove with purpose. I wondered why we were going all the way to Philadelphia, but every time I looked at her, she shushed me. The next thing I knew the valet at the fancy Bellevue Hotel was opening my door, and Aunt Lenora was quickly guiding me into Tiffany & Co. "Happy graduation!" she exclaimed. "Pick any piece of jewelry you want." I felt shocked and then, in quick succession, special, and loved, and beautiful.

After some gentle prodding from Aunt Lenora and the salesperson, I selected an Elsa Peretti bean necklace on an enhancer, partially because it was packaged in a suede jewelry box I had seen in the movie *Pretty Woman*, and this felt like my *Pretty Woman* moment. The day ended with us relishing chocolate fondue at the restaurant on the top floor of the Bellevue, my necklace sparkling for all to see, and my fingers reaching up every few moments to make sure it was still there.

It was still there. It is still here. And now Aunt Lenora's three-year-old granddaughter, my lovely goddaughter, delights in wearing it and hearing the story behind it. Aunt Lenora teaches her too, not formally in the classroom, but just as importantly at home. I tell her just how much she has to look forward to—that the teaching never ends. Just last year, Aunt Lenora reminded me of the importance of believing in myself, reminded me that she believed in me, and convinced me to take one of the biggest risks of my life, leaving my corporate job and doing what made me happiest—becoming a teacher.

Aimee Cirucci has written about everything from bad bosses to book clubs for a variety of online and print publications. Thanks to her aunt's encouragement, she also teaches in the strategic and organizational communications program at Temple University. For more information, visit her Web site at *http://cirucci.com*.

No Rest for the Weary

Tammy Stone

"Okay, everybody up! Hands in the air. Wiggle your fingers. Now, jumping jacks. Let's go, let's go!"

This was weird. No one had ever made us do this before.

"Now run around the room. That's right. *Un, deux, trois, marche!* The limber soul feeds on the acreages of flexed bodies and youthful mileage. Listen to the music of your mind. Let it take you to the reaches of . . ."

Huh?

"Breaking into a little sweat yet? Good, then it's time to begin. Take your seats, my charges, and we will commence discussions with an exploration of the unique lavatory systems of ancient Babylonia."

This was the first day of eighth grade, and we had heard the rumors about Mr. Murray Wilson. At our conservative private school in Nepean, Ontario, he had a reputation for shaking things up. He had wild blue eyes, untamed salt-and-pepper hair, and he dressed defiantly, wearing mismatched clothing that rebelled against the silent, but obvious, teachers' dress code: scuffed shoes, multicolored sweaters, and faded blazers with patchwork on the elbows. He spoke eight different languages and was clearly brilliant, but— even when speaking English—his words tumbled out of his mouth so fast and furiously that what he was trying to convey often remained wholly obtuse.

He launched the year with a diagrammed presentation on the archaic and arcane toilets of the Middle East, and quickly followed with an idea that we should perform a bilingual— French and English—play based on an eighteenth-century explorer from the hinterlands of Quebec, Canada. And this wasn't just any play. When he pulled reams of paper out of his briefcase, he informed us that the manuscript, covered with shorthand, doodles, and scrawls, was his original work. The play, like Mr. Wilson, was brilliant, complex, and way above our heads. Even though his ingenious use of words enthralled us, even after three readings, we didn't really understand the convoluted plot twists and dense, complex dialogue.

Throughout the year, Mr. Wilson worked to expand our repertoire. The other eighth-grade class read *Anne Frank: The Diary of a Young Girl* and answered questions like, "How would you describe Anne's relationship with her sister?" Mr. Wilson aimed higher, insisting we tackle Shakespeare's *The Tempest*. "We're not supposed to read Shakespeare until high school!" we all wailed. But Mr. Wilson was not deterred—he always felt confident we could reach a bit further, and then further still. Thanks to him, we learned to spot a pun long before we knew what puns were. We learned the beauty of language and how a brilliant author could magically weave words and images together to create great works of art.

One morning after limbering up with yoga exercises—another novel experience that he lured us into doing and about which we knew little—Mr. Wilson instructed us to line up by the row of windows that looked out onto a quiet street.

"Okay, you can start writing now," he said.

"Write what?" We looked at one another, wondering if we had forgotten to do a homework assignment. We knew the other class had just finished the standard "What I did over the long weekend" compositions.

"Look out the window. Describe what you see."

We were stumped. All we saw was the same manicured grass, bare trees, and stolid brick buildings we saw every single day.

"What's there to write about?" we asked in unison. "Nothing's happening."

"Sure there is; look closer." He silently gazed out the window.

I remember thinking he was nuts and fantasizing about hatching an escape plan with Ilan, who had become the focus of my romantic yearning, when a tottering, older woman came into view. She was dressed like an aristocratic lady and walked with a cane, which created an excruciatingly slow gait. Although I didn't see a real story, it suddenly dawned on me: *Something* is happening. I was standing at a window in perfect health, with my entire life about to open up, watching another person, with severe limitations, struggle through the final stage of her life. I suddenly realized that I could use my imagination to create a story about what might happen if our lives converged. My stomach fluttered with excitement.

When I turned in my story, Mr. Wilson applauded my efforts. I loved the glimmer in his eyes when he said, "Well done, Ms. Stone."

In the coming months, his use of kooky ideas to spur imagination helped me see endless possibilities for flushing out stories. After he played a symphonic masterpiece and asked us to imagine a story—and I created a tragic romantic tale about tormented love between a man and woman—Mr. Wilson told me I was destined to become a writer. And I felt a thrill that rushed all the way through me. The genius with high expectations thought I had potential, real potential!

It never occurred to us to wonder why Mr. Wilson chose to teach snotty-nosed, bratty kids. Years later, I discovered he was concurrently working toward his doctorate in literature; writing plays, and poems, and novels; and organizing writing and poetry evenings in the community. And lucky for us, he dedicated his life to teaching, offering up his unique ability to see through our defensive blustering, complaints, and resistance. He not only successfully steered us through that awkward—yet sublimely open—period of adolescent becoming, he ignited our curiosity, fostered our creativity, and expanded our horizons.

Once, during spring break from university, I snuck back unannounced to watch him in action. And there he was, as always, leading the class in jumping jacks, ignoring their whining, and grinning from ear to ear. When he saw me peering around the doorway, he enthusiastically waved me in.

"Ladies and gentlemen," he said, bowing toward me, "Ms. Stone was one of my star pupils." He paused to turn to the class. "And I believe we shall ask her to honor us with a recital from the Shakespearean sonnet both she and you have learned in this room."

My heart skipped a beat, but one did not deny Mr. Wilson, particularly when his impish smile lit up the room. To my surprise, a stanza I had not spoken for seven years tumbled out.

"Ah, that's lovely," he said, placing a hand over his heart. "Ms. Stone, will you please share what it is you want to do with your life?"

"I'm not sure," I said, pausing to notice that he was already beaming. "As you so skillfully taught me, the world is my oyster, and it's wise to keep my options open. I haven't narrowed down my choices yet, but as you also taught me, writing is a tremendous way to not only make sense of things, but to do the noblest of things—to stay connected to my heart and spirit."

Mr. Wilson clapped his hands together and nodded his head knowingly. He had done his job, and he had done it beautifully.

Tammy Stone lives in Toronto, Canada, where she works for the Toronto International Film Festival Group. She has had her freelance work published in newspapers and magazines internationally. She's currently working on a collection of short stories and her first novel.

Winning Isn't Everything

Chris Jensen

Football is a violently physical, demanding game that involves almost as much mental strength as physical endurance. Even for high school, we worked out long before the season began and long after it ended. In the summer, we exercised outside, often grinding out wind sprints in 100-degree, muggy Missouri summers. We'd run long and hard, until the sweat swung off our arms and faces, and then we'd do one more sprint, then another, and then another. In the winter, we lifted weights for hours, until our muscles burned and shook, and then we'd add weights and lift until we crumbled. Coach would always be there, reminding us that our archrivals—the boys in Chillicothe—were hot on our tails.

Coach Naylor won 234 games at Marshall High School in thirty-five years—good for fifth-best all-time in Missouri high school football. He won one state championship and eleven conference titles. In his whole high school career, his team lost only one homecoming game. His reputation for perfection and effort was legendary. Yeah, Coach was one tough bird.

On the field, he wasn't afraid to get right in a young man's face and tell him exactly what he thought. When I missed a block, his tongue-lashing would always sting. I would lift myself off the turf, pull a chunk of Gregg-Mitchell sod from my headgear, and look over to where Coach would invariably be jumping up and down on the sideline, salivating at the chance to let me know up close and personal that my actions just cost us a potential touchdown. Man, that twenty-yard jog to the bench always seemed like miles. My legs would suddenly feel like lead weights, as though I were running in the shallow end of the swimming pool—each stride had its own resistance to overcome.

When I reached the sidelines, Coach would barrel toward me with amazing speed, his large form growing bigger by the second, his jaws clenched. He'd shove his nose right up against my facemask repeatedly and shout so vigorously his spit showered my face. "Dang it, Jensen! You have to block him! You don't block him, we don't go anywhere!"

Although not widely known, Coach wasn't always so prickly. Luckily, I experienced his softer side. My allegiance to him actually dated back to a crisp, Midwestern autumn day before my freshman season had even begun. The weekend prior, my family had visited my grandmother, Naomi Queen, in Tabor,

Iowa. Mimi had moved into a nursing home, and when we arrived, she didn't remember my mother, my dad, my eight-year old sister Julie, or me. I was devastated. We all were.

On the way home, even though it was a bright, sunny, gorgeous fall day, my mother muffled sobs for the entire five-hour drive. I stared out the car window as row after row of tall cornfields blurred past, not saying much, just listening to the sound of my mother sobbing—which would haunt me for years—and wiping away salty tears when they crashed onto my lips. How did this happen? How could Mimi know us two months ago, and suddenly not know us at all?

The next day, when it came time to don my practice clothes, I tried to suck it up. I didn't want the older team members to see me crying. But when Coach Naylor walked by and casually asked how I was doing, to my horror, tears sprung out of my eyes. I didn't want our tough coach to see me cry! Surely he'd think I was a wimpy freshman, someone he had to coddle. I tried to choke back the tears and buck up, but I just couldn't. All the emotions I'd held in the check on that drive home exploded, full speed, catching me off guard and defenseless.

To my surprise, Coach sat down and wrapped his strong arm around me so tightly his thick heavy hand gripped my other shoulder. The combined strength and gentleness in his touch made me cry more. And so we sat, wordless for several minutes, staring at my opened locker, where my combination lock dangled undone. I felt like that lock—broken wide open.

When words came, I explained the situation with Mimi. "I just don't get it, Coach. Last time I visited her, she knew me.

Now, she doesn't know me; she doesn't know her own child; she doesn't know any of us. I don't understand," I said, shaking my head mournfully.

"Sometimes, as people get older, they forget names, places, things that happened in their lives. Even though it doesn't seem possible, it's not that unusual for them not to remember people close to them—people who have been important to them their entire lives," Coach, said, and then paused to give my shoulder another squeeze. "It has a name; it's called dementia. And it's hard, but harder on the family. She doesn't mean to forget you. She has no control over it, and the sad fact is that we don't know why it happens or what to do about it. It's a tough break, Jensen."

The moment passed, and I went on to experience that harsher side of Coach. His coaching was legendary, and his tough methods effective, but on that autumn day, Coach and I formed a special relationship. Rather than grabbing me by the helmet to show me how men go after what they want, he grabbed me by my heart and showed me how a young man grieves. He didn't tell me to suck it up; he sat down beside me and made me feel like it was his Mimi, too. I could tell him everything and not be ashamed of my pain or my tears. He accepted me and gave me strength when I had none. I learned a lot about what it meant to be a man that day, sitting by that yellow locker with its combination lock dangling.

I learned that the true sign of man is not how macho he is—it's his ability to listen, be compassionate, and be gentle with other people's feelings. And it doesn't matter if you're a tough-guy coach who molded teams that won 234 football games or only lost one homecoming game. A true test of a man is whether he can help one boy sort out his feelings when he's hurting beyond belief and feels overcome with confusion and sadness that his Mimi is gone.

Chris Jensen attended the University of Missouri-Columbia on a football scholarship, where he was an inside linebacker, fullback and tight end for the Tigers. He earned a bachelor's degree in broadcast journalism and a master's degree in communication, and he worked as broadcaster before becoming a model and actor, appearing regularly in television commercials. He lives in Atlanta, Georgia, with his wife, Christine, and son, Larson.

Lessons in Hue

Karen J. Coates

When I was little I loved to play school, teaching make-believe pupils seated alphabetically in rows of imaginary desks. I made lesson plans for math and science, reading and penmanship. I corrected imaginary papers and distributed imaginary grades. My made-up classroom contained books and blackboards, board games and puzzles. I taught one-hour classes, and permitted recess after lunch; my mother's kitchen served as our mess hall.

I had clear ideas about scholastic order: Teachers taught; students learned. Those were the lines. It would take me a while to understand that, in real life, the lines often blurred.

Many years later, I spent a semester in Vietnam with six other American graduate students, each of us with internships in international relations. We had journeyed to Hanoi to learn about all things

Vietnamese. But soon after we landed, our Vietnamese colleagues assessed our one key skill—English fluency—and determined that we were qualified to teach English. We were experts, they said. We knew English; they wanted to learn; therefore, we must teach—right now.

With virtually no time to prepare, my American partner and I stood at the front of a conference-room-turned-classroom in a breezy building that housed the Vietnam Women's Museum. We were there to teach the guides. Rows and rows of women in silk *ao dais* eagerly watched our mouths and traced our words as we burbled phrases in feeble attempts to master this impromptu job.

The students called us *co*, an endearment for teacher. Our class worked beautifully, twice a week, for three months. We practiced grammar, vocabulary, and pronunciation—things that would be useful to the women while leading foreigners through aisles and displays depicting the Vietnamese woman's role in their society—as mothers of their country and sisters to the revolution. We also recited Vietnamese legends, which began as exercises in English for our students, but morphed into studies of Vietnamese culture for us. We taught them about the English language; they taught us about Vietnamese life.

When we spoke to the class, our students mimicked our words in perfect pitch, inflection, and pace. Their singsong voices surprised us. They sang our words just as they would their own, employing their native tonal tongues. We raised our voices; they raised their voices. We spoke abruptly; they spoke abruptly. They taught us how to listen more carefully. We were all teachers and all students, all the same.

A few years later, I took my husband, Jerry, to Vietnam. We visited Hue, a crumbling city in the middle of Vietnam's protracted north-south stretch. Hue had served as the country's political capital for 140 years, but it was badly crushed in the American war. Jerry and I rented a couple of rusty bikes and pedaled into the verdant fields to do a little casual exploring.

A stranger quickly approached. He wanted help with his English, a common request in Vietnam, but Jerry and I simply were not in the mood. For weeks, we had felt swamped in traffic, buzzed by the noise of big cities, and wiped by the seasonal heat. That day, we simply wanted to be alone. I told the stranger we were going for a bike ride, hoping to discourage him.

"I go by bike, too," he replied. "You pay no money to me. I know many temples." He would guide, we would talk, and he would learn—that was his plan. And, without any encouragement or any recognition that we wanted him to tag along, he pedaled beside us for quite some time.

The man said he wanted to show us tombs, enunciating the "b." We corrected his pronunciation, but again declined his invitation, turning our rickety wheels in another direction. Yet when I shifted my head a few minutes later, the man was back, pedaling beside me again. "Okay, okay!" I said, finally motioning for him to follow. We would let him ride with us to the tomb of Thieu Tri, an emperor who had ruled more than 150 years.

The stranger's name was Long. He dressed neatly in a white dress shirt tucked into green work pants and an American-style baseball cap. He was thirty-one, short and bony, with crossed eyes. When he discovered I spoke some Vietnamese, his face beamed and he immediately defined the boundaries of our relationship, calling me *co*—teacher—and himself *em*—student or child.

When we reached the ruins, we parked our bikes and walked through rows of pillars on a dilapidated bridge over murky ponds until we reached a stone wall shrouded in jungle foliage that circled the tombs. Long had pulled out a pen and tissue scraps, and began writing down everything we said as we chatted. He could not read English, but since Vietnamese shares the same alphabet, he knew the letters, though not the sounds. So as we talked and the sound of the words reached his ears, Long recorded the letters phonetically and grouped them to tonally match his native Vietnamese.

Then Long told us about the Minh Mang tomb, across the Perfume River, "where tourists go." He wanted to take us.

"Many tourists go by boat to the temple," I said, slowly offering Long a line to repeat and record. In his studious hands, Long's phonetic rendition of the sentence became, "Me ni tua rit gau bau bot to dit tem bo."

We took our bikes to a spot where locals crossed the river by sampan. Long bargained a price with the boss. On the other side, we disembarked and pedaled deeper into the steaming afternoon—uphill and downhill, farther and farther, toward the famed Minh Mang tomb.

Once there, the three of us wandered through the gardens and sat on the stone base of a temple where Long recounted his family's story in broken English. "Father for me was military

American," he said, and I gently repeated: "My father fought along with the Americans."

Long wrote fervently, equating the letter X with the sound "s." Jerry and I listened further to his story, and then we taught him another string of sentences, which he repeated: "The Hanoi government put my father in prison. My father was in prison for six years. When the Hanoi government came, I stopped school."

We also learned that the government had imprisoned Long's grandmother because she fought on the American side. Some of Long's family had fled to the United States, but he never did "because I married very early and the government would not let me go."

We sat there, the three of us, dangling our feet from a platform in ruins. Suddenly, I realized I was no longer cranky. I was no longer hot and no longer impatient. I no longer wished to be alone. I wanted more and more to learn from Long. And I realized, peering across ancient promenades and artistic pavilions, that my impatience had almost made me miss this opportunity to be Long's *em.*

As we left the tomb and found the road again, and the three of us worked our way down the hill, back toward Hue, Long stopped abruptly in the empty street.

"I'm sorry. I need an English book. I have no money. Can you help me?"

Jerry stuck his hands into his pocket and brought out a wad of *dong*—spare change, just a dollar or two, but enough to bring a misting of tears to Long's eyes. "Thank you," he said.

"I have no money. I have two kids. I want to learn, but I have no teacher." He smiled and shook Jerry's hand, then bowed to both of us.

Then he turned and rode into the hills, where he tilled his fields, where he raised his kids, where he had no classroom but eagerly studied English from English-speaking tourists and whatever he could write on scraps of tissue. He rode off into the sunset both *co* and *em*, as were we—all teachers and all students, all the same.

Karen J. Coates is author of *Cambodia Now: Life in the Wake of War*. She fell in love with Vietnam and has since spent the better part of a decade covering Asia for publications around the world. Read more of her writings at *http://redcoates.net* and *http://ramblingspoon.com/blog*.

The Greatest Teacher of All

Susan Reynolds

I've had memorable teachers. Even though I can't remember his name—my brother Roy would remember—a music teacher in seventh grade opened my eyes and ears to classical music. My family never played Beethoven, Bach, or Mozart, so the first time this teacher set the stage—by taking us to the auditorium, asking us to lay our heads back, close our eyes, and envision a sailboat crossing the ocean, or wind blowing tree leaves across an open field, or a camel approaching from a distant desert hill—and then dropped the needle on Ravel's Bolero, I wept. An appreciation for classical music was birthed, a life changed.

Mrs. Charlotte Jewart, my tenth-grade English teacher, taught me how to read, interpret, and relish Shakespeare. She had had my older brother and sister before me, so she forewarned me from day one that she expected big things. "You can do better," she would always say, peering over her glasses. I'd work harder on the next essay, and the next, and the next, but I never got above a B-plus. "You can do better," she'd admonish, and I would groan and go home complaining. I was an A student, and I *was* working hard.

This pattern went on all year, so at the end I spent months researching my subject, and then writing, rewriting, rewriting, and rewriting my final paper. It was sublime, my swan song to Mrs. Jewart. When I handed it to her, I grinned. Two days later I had it back with the long desired and hard-won A-plus. I never rested on my laurels or took the easy way out again. Thanks partly to Mrs. Jewart, I built a successful career in journalism without obtaining a degree in either English or journalism. I did so by marshalling my intelligence, researching in depth, being absolutely thorough when compiling facts, and then writing, rewriting, and rewriting every story I worked on.

Years later, my son had a fabulous, life-changing teacher. Brett was entering fourth grade a shy, overly sensitive boy whose self-imposed perfectionism was painful to observe. He was terrified to break any rules, to be less than perfect—seemingly locked into an idea that rigid adherence would keep his parents from divorcing, his world from unraveling.

Luckily, Mr. Peters at Brown's Valley Elementary School in the Napa Valley not only walked into my son's life, he blasted his way into it, and by doing so engaged my son's curiosity, enthusiasm, intelligence, imagination, and energy.

One day, quite spontaneously, Mr. Peters told his students to push their desks to the sides of the room and then led them in a day spent laying railroad tracks and creating a village out of whatever they could find. Mr. Peters then donned an engineer's cap and ran around the room, pumping his arms up and down, *wooing* as loud as a train whistles. When the principal came down the hall and peered in the door window, Mr. Peters tipped his cap and kept running and wooing. My son came home ecstatic but looked at me as if he half expected me to express dismay. I was thrilled and told him so.

When Mr. Peters took his class out whale watching, he told them spewing over the sides of the rails was fun and demonstrated the method, complete with a wobbly-kneed dash to the rail, outrageous sound effects, and hysterical facial gestures. They laughed too hard to notice the ocean swells. But their day wasn't over. On the way home, they stopped at a Mexican restaurant, where he double-dog dared them to put a whole hot pepper into their mouths, chew it for two full minutes, and then swallow it. My son—who ate only chicken, pizza, and hamburgers, and never, never, never anything remotely spicy or hot—stood in line, along with all twenty-five students, and chewed that pepper until tears ran down his cheeks from the heat. They would do anything to make Mr. Peters proud.

Mr. Peters's students learned everything they were supposed to learn, but Brett also learned how to be spontaneous, goofy, irreverent, and playful. His creativity blossomed, and he had a renewed sense of *joie de vivre*. One day when straddling second base during Little League practice, for no particular reason, my son plopped down on the base and tossed his cap in the air, laughing hysterically. The coach was not amused, but I stood up and did a happy dance because Brett had crossed that crucial line from rigid conformance to screwing up occasionally. I wrote Mr. Peters a long, passionate, mushy, sentimental love letter at the end of the year. He saved my son's life.

So I know good teachers, and I hold all of them in my heart. But the teacher I most admire in the world is one whose classroom I have never visited and whose students I do not know. I do know that he is dedicated, persistent, patient, kind, funny, and loving. I know that he really wanted to be a rock star and after spending many years chasing that dream, and then many years teaching elementary school, went back to school to earn a master's degree in special education instead.

At the time, he was raising two teenage stepsons and his young daughter. His wife had a more demanding and more financially successful job, but he opted to continue teaching elementary school because his school in Florida consistently had boys facing emotional or learning challenges, and he had a gift for working with them. He had even taken in a very troubled young girl and struggled for years to give her the solid, healthy family she so desperately needed. When he had to surrender, it tortured him. He's a sucker for kids that get left behind.

In Florida, male elementary school teachers are few and underpaid. Other men rarely look up to them or envy them, and they can't afford fancy cars or spiffy suits or exotic vacations. Most of the time, they are scrambling to pay bills and working steadily, if painfully slowly, toward building a retirement fund. These days they don't know if that pension will be there at the end, or if they'll have that health care the administrators held out as a carrot for accepting lower pay. When it comes to societal status, male elementary school teachers are often hidden in the shadows or low on the totem pole. And now this teacher works surrounded by young women just out of college who tell him he's absolutely adorable. He is absolutely adorable, and energetic, and dedicated, and grossly underappreciated in our larger society.

This teacher knows all that, and he complains occasionally, but more often he'll grin and tell you that he gets huge paychecks all the time. Year after year after year, former students come back to thank him. They write him letters and they call and they send cards, and their parents also come to thank him. The school now gives him all the problem students, those who haven't passed the basic minimum requirements to graduate to the next level. Everyone else has thrown up their hands, but this teacher does what he does so well that he turns every one of them around. By the end of the year, all his students pass the tests they need to pass—*and* they can read and write and think and feel good about themselves because this teacher cared enough to give his all to them.

He's a fabulous teacher—the best—and I know because he's my brother, Roy Joseph Reynolds, and I am so, so proud of him.

Susan Reynolds is a freelance writer and author. She has authored three nonfiction books and is currently editing Adams Media's *Hero* series. Whenever possible she showers her brother, Roy Reynolds, with the accolades he deserves. Learn more about Susan's work on *http:// literarycottage.com*.